How do you do

Edition CS

Stage Two

On the move

Textbook

Herausgegeben von Eric Orton und Peter H. Stoldt

Ferdinand Schöningh

42920

Englisches Unterrichtswerk für die Hauptschule
(für das 6. Schuljahr)

Autoren

Eric Orton, Head of Modern Languages, Royal Grammar School, Worcester (Texts, Drills)
Rudolf Höppner, Studienleiter für Englisch am Seminar für Gymnasien, Lübeck (Grammar, Phonetics)
Jürgen Kienzler, Realschullehrer, Ludwigsburg (Exercises)
Gottfried Kumpf, Realschullehrer, Ludwigsburg (Exercises)

Berater

Winfried Bürling, Hauptschulkonrektor und Seminarleiter für Englisch, Bottrop
Karin Ebbighausen, Pädagogische Hochschule, Ludwigsburg
Peter von Esebeck, Hauptschulrektor, Braunschweig
Trude Nonner, Erz. Wiss. Fakultät, Universität Regensburg
Peter H. Stoldt, Oberschulrat, Bremen
Ute Rampillon, R.P.Z. Bad Kreuznach

Verlagsredaktion

Lyndy Macready
Christine Smith
Gerald Williams

Illustratoren

Bill Burnard
Heinz-Joachim Draeger
David Lock
Gisela Könemund

München · Wien · Zürich
Printed in Germany
Herstellung: Ferdinand Schöningh, Paderborn
ISBN 3-506-42920-5

Contents

R = Revision Unit

Unit 1

a

Say 'cheese'

1

Eight boys and nine girls from Hamburg are on the **boat** from Hamburg to Harwich.

2

It is a lovely day.
They can already see the English **coast.**

3

They want to **visit** their English **penfriends** in Worcester.

4

Their teachers, Herr Henning and Frau Schmidt, are taking a **photograph** of the **group.**

5

"Say 'cheese'. Good. Thank you."

Questions

1 How many boys and girls are there on the boat? Where is the boat going to?
2 What can they see?
3 Where do their pen-friends live?
4 Who are their two teachers? What are the two teachers doing?

Can you complete this?

1

Herr Henning and Frau Schmidt are on the ... from ... to ...

2

They are taking a ... of the ...

3

They can see the English ...

b The English coast

English girl: Excuse me, do you know where we are now? Is that the coast over there?

Carsten: I'm sorry. I don't understand. My English isn't very good yet. What's "coast"? Can you please repeat your question?

Girl: Is that the English coast? Is that England?

Carsten: Now I understand. Yes, I think so. That must be Harwich. It's half past six now.

Girl: Thank you. I think your English is great!

Questions

1 What is over there?
2 Who can't understand?
3 Are they near the German coast?
4 What is the name of the town on the coast?
5 What is the time?
6 Is Carsten's English awful?

On the ferry

On the ferry and on his first day in England, Carsten can't understand a lot of English. So he says: "Please don't talk so fast." And then: "Please repeat your question."

Auf der Fähre und während des ersten Tages in England kann Carsten noch nicht viel Englisch verstehen, da die Leute so schnell sprechen.

Man: Is that the English coast?
Carsten: I'm sorry I don't understand.
Can you please repeat your question?
Man: Is that the English coast?
Carsten: Now I understand. Yes, it is.

Partner Work

Now talk to your partner. Sprich jetzt mit deinem Partner.

Man: Is that Harwich?
Carsten: I'm sorry, I don't ...
Can you please repeat your ...?
Man: Is that ...?
Carsten: Now I ... Yes, it is.

Man: Is that your pen-friend?
Carsten: I'm sorry, I ...
Man: Is that ...?
Carsten: Now ... No, he isn't.

Man: Is that your teacher?
Carsten: I'm sorry ...
Can you ...?
Man: Is ...?
Carsten: Now ... Yes ...

Man: Is that the boat from Harwich to Bremerhaven?
Carsten: I'm ...
Man: Is ...?
Carsten: Now ... Yes ...

Go on:

the cafeteria	a waiter
London	the post office
the headmaster	the dining-room
a farm	the fridge

C On Harwich Station

1 The pupils from Hamburg are on Harwich station now.
They are standing with their **suitcases** on **platform** 1.

2 There the **boat-train** is waiting.

3 A **porter** is just showing Frau Schmidt her **seat** in **coach** 10.

4 This is the **dining-car.**

5 A waiter is **serving** breakfast in the dining-car.

6 Now it is half past seven. The boat-train is leaving the station.

Find the correct sentences

1 The pupils from Hamburg	...is waiting at platform 1.
2 The boat-train	...breakfast in the dining-car.
3 A porter is just showing	...half past seven.
4 A waiter is serving	...Frau Schmidt her seat.
5 Now it is	...are on Harwich station now.

Questions

1 Where are the pupils standing?
2 Is the boat-train leaving now?
3 Where is Frau Schmidt's seat?
4 Where do you have breakfast on a train?
5 What is the waiter doing now?
6 At what time is the boat-train leaving Harwich station?

Can you complete this?

Two boys are taking their ... to ... 10. The ... is waiting. A ... is carrying Frau Schmidt's ... Her ... is in ... 9. The ... is in front of coach 9. A ... is ... breakfast in the dining-car.

suitcase serving platform waiter seat boat-train dining-car coach

d Breakfast in the dining-car

Frau Schmidt: Do you want bacon and eggs, Carsten?
Or do you just want toast?
Carsten: Oh, bacon and eggs, please.
Frau Schmidt: And you, Helga?
Helga: Just toast for me, please. I don't like big breakfasts.
Frau Schmidt: What do you want, Klaus?
Do you like big English breakfasts?
Klaus: Yes, I do. I'd like bacon and eggs too, please.
Frau Schmidt: And do you want tea or coffee?
All: Tea, please!
Frau Schmidt: All right. Waiter!
Waiter: Yes, madam?
Frau Schmidt: Three bacon and eggs, one toast, and four cups of tea, please.

Questions

1 Carsten wants bacon and eggs. Do you like bacon and eggs, too?
2 Helga just wants toast. Do you like toast, too?
3 Klaus wants tea. Do you like tea, too?
4 Do they all want coffee?

First breakfast in England

Now we are in the dining-car. The boys and girls from Germany are having their first breakfast in England. A waiter is serving breakfast.

Waiter: Do you want cornflakes or fruit-juice?
You: Give me the fruit-juice, please.
Waiter: Do you want biscuits or toast?
You: Give me the biscuits, please.

Partner work

Now talk to your neighbour:

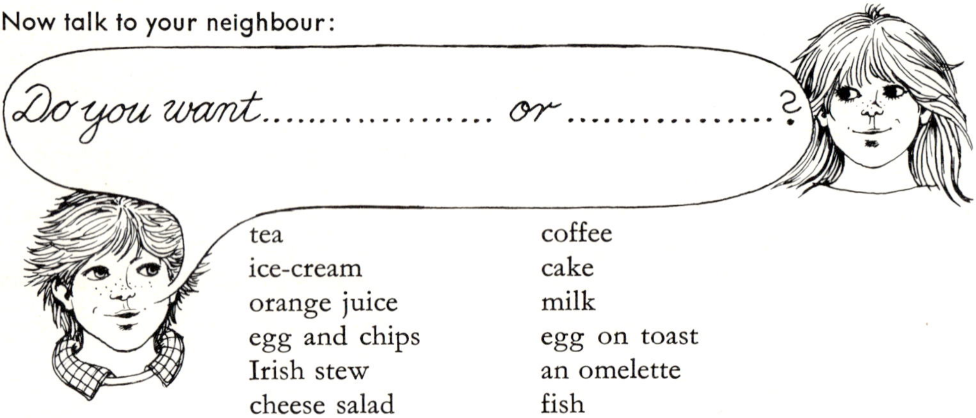

tea	coffee
ice-cream	cake
orange juice	milk
egg and chips	egg on toast
Irish stew	an omelette
cheese salad	fish
lemonade	tea

e Liverpool Street Station, London

1 *Frau Schmidt:* What's the matter, Gisela? Why are you **crying**?
Gisela: I can't find my **wallet**.

2 *Frau Schmidt:* Oh, dear. Do you know how much money is in it?
Gisela: Yes, of course. All my **pocket-money**: £20 and DM 30. I need that money.

3 *Carsten:* Look, there's an **enquiry office** over there. Let's **ask about** your wallet.

Frau Schmidt: All right, Carsten. Go and ask. Gisela can stay here.

4 *Carsten:* Excuse me, can you help me? My friend can't find her wallet. Perhaps ...

Porter: Well, go to the Lost Property Office beside platform 9.

5 *Porter:* **Explain everything** to the **clerk** there. He can help you.

Five minutes later

6 *Clerk at the Lost Property Office:* A brown wallet, you say? The **ticket-collector** here has got a brown wallet. Is this it? Good.

7 *Carsten:* Are you **happy** now, Gisela?

Gisela: Thank you very much, Carsten. Yes, I am. You're wonderful. Your English must be very good.

8 *Carsten:* Well, — it's **useful**, very useful. I can see that.

Questions

1 Who is crying?
Why is she crying?
3 How much English money is in her wallet?
4 Where is the Lost Property Office?
5 Who can help Carsten at the Lost Property Office?
What must Carsten do there?
6 Who has got Gisela's wallet in his hand?
7 Is Gisela still crying now?
What is Carsten's English like?

Ursula can't find her wallet

Ursula always has to look for something. In England she doesn't take care of her things either. She doesn't know what to do. So she asks someone.

Ursula sucht immer etwas. Auch in England paßt sie auf ihre Sachen nicht auf. Da sie sich nicht auskennt, muß sie jemand um Rat fragen.

Grammar Practice

1 A do — don't

a) **Do** you like big English breakfasts? **Yes, I do.**

b) **Do** you want toast? **No, I don't.**

? → do

1	I like bacon and eggs.	**Do** you like bacon and eggs?
2	I want tea.	**Do** you want . . . ?
3	I like big English breakfasts.	**Do** . . . ?
4	I want lemonade.	. . . ?
5	I like ice-cream.	. . . ?

1 B Make sentences

do + not → don't

1 I **don't** want coffee.
2 . . . **don't** like Irish stew.
3 . . . want milk.
4 . . . like cake.
5 . . . want an omelette.

Do you . . . . . . ?

1 C Answer some questions

Answer the questions with "**don't**"

1	Do you want sausages?	No, I **don't.**
2	Do you like chocolate?	No, I . . .
3	Do you want apple juice?	. . .
4	Do you like egg and chips?	. . .
5	Do you want beer?	. . .

Now answer with "**do**" or "**don't**"

1	Do you want toast?	Yes, I . . .
2	Do you like coffee?	No, I . . .
3	Do you like English breakfasts?	Yes, I . . .
4	Do you want bacon and eggs?	No, I . . .
5	Do you like salads?	Yes, I . . .

Exercises

1 In the dining-car

a) Ask your neighbour:

You: Do you like tea?

...cornflakes?
...milk?
...hot coffee?
...omelettes?
...cold lemonade?
...ice-cream?
...cake?
...orange juice?
...egg and chips?
...Irish stew?

Your friend: Yes I do. / No, I don't.

b) Now you are a waiter. You work in the dining-car. You ask the boys and girls at the tables.

Waiter: Do you want tea?
Tom: Yes, we do. / No, we don't.

Look at Exercise 1a and ask some more questions.

2 Do you remember ...?
The Menu

You are looking at the menu. You want to know what your friend likes.

Du hast die Speisekarte in der Hand und möchtest wissen, was Dein Freund gern ißt.

a) Ask your friend:

You: Do you like ...
Your friend: Yes, I do. / No, I don't.
I love ... / I hate ...

An die Eltern

Seit einem Jahr arbeitet Ihr Kind mit HOW DO YOU DO. Wir hoffen, es macht ihm Spaß. Im zweiten Lernjahr begleiten wir eine Schülergruppe nach England. Die Kinder übernachten in der Londoner Jugendherberge, kaufen in der Oxford Street ein und werden als Gäste in englische Familien aufgenommen. Sprechfertigkeit und Hörverstehen stehen im Vordergrund. Wie im ersten Lernjahr wird das Lernen durch Tonbandaufnahmen und Bildgeschichten besonders gefördert. Den Unterricht können Sie zu Hause mit Hilfe der Schülercassetten sinnvoll ergänzen. Diese Cassetten enthalten die wichtigsten Dialoge des Textbooks zum Hören und Nachsprechen, und sie helfen Ihrem Kind,seine Aussprache ständig zu verbessern, die englische Sprache leichter zu verstehen und anzuwenden.

HOW DO YOU DO CS/2

Schüler-Cassette 1	Best.-Nr. 62927	DM 18,—*
Schüler-Cassette 2	Best.-Nr. 62928	DM 18,—*
Schüler-Cassette 3	Best.-Nr. 62929	DM 18,—*
Schüler-Cassette 4	Best.-Nr. 62930	DM 18,—*

*Unverbindlicher empfohlener Preis Stand: 1. 4. 1979. Preisänderungen vorbehalten

Bestellkarte

Ich bestelle zur festen Lieferung direkt an die unten genannte Anschrift oder über die umseitig angegebene Firma:

HOW DO YOU DO CS/2

__________ Schüler-Cassette 1 Best.-Nr. 62927

__________ Schüler-Cassette 2 Best.-Nr. 62928

__________ Schüler-Cassette 3 Best.-Nr. 62929

__________ Schüler-Cassette 4 Best.-Nr. 62930

Name

Straße Ort (mit Postleitzahl)

Datum Unterschrift (des Erziehungsberechtigten)

Erfüllungsort: Paderborn

Absender

Erbitte Lieferung über die Firma

Buchhandlung

Straße

Ort

Bitte als
Postkarte
frankieren

POSTKARTE

Ferdinand Schöningh
Jühenplatz am Rathaus
Postfach 2540

D-4790 Paderborn

b) Your friend asks:

Your friend: How much is/are ...
You: It's ... They are ...

c) Tom und Peter haben schrecklichen Hunger, aber wenig Geld. Sie befinden sich im Golden Egg Restaurant. Tom hat eine Speisekarte und liest Peter vor. Peter, der das Geld hat, interessiert sich zuerst einmal für die Preise:

Tom: Do you like egg and chips?
Peter: Yes, I do. I love it.
How much are egg and chips?
Tom: They're 80p.
Peter: That's OK.

Look at the menu on page 16 and act the scene with your partner: "Do you like ..."

3 Can you ask questions?

Die Austauschschüler befinden sich nun bei ihren Gastfamilien und gehen in die englische Schule. Dort werden sie von den englischen Schülern ausgefragt.

Do you speak English?
Do you like England?
Do you like Irish stew?
... eat cornflakes every morning?
... learn French?
... help your father in the afternoon?
... wash your hands in the morning?
... like apples?
... hate cake?
... clean your shoes every day?
...?

Yes, I do.
Yes, I do.
No, I don't. I hate Irish stew.
...
...
...
...
...
...
...
...

4 Do you know the answers?

1 Do teachers clean schools?
2 Do waiters serve tea?
3 Do reporters interview headmasters?
4 Do drivers work in the garden?
5 Do hairdressers wash your hair?
6 Do policemen interview reporters?

2 HDYD CS 2 Textbook 42920

5 Tim's wallet

Can you complete this? Use the correct form of the verb.

Example: Tim (run) ... to the Lost Property Office.
Tim **runs** to the Lost Property Office.

There he (explain) ... everything. The clerk (write) ... it all down. Then he (ask) ... a porter.
Five minutes later, a ticket collector (come in) ... and (give) ... Tim his wallet. Tim (thank) ... the ticket collector. The ticket collector (say) ...: "That's all right."

6 A picture story

Mother is busy

Example:
work: kitchen
Every morning at 8 o'clock she ...
Every morning at 8 o'clock she **works in the kitchen.**

1

eat: apple
Fifteen minutes later she ...

2

clean: dining-room
Then she ...

3

drink: tea
One hour later she ...

4

write: shopping-list
Then she ...

5

work: garden
Later she ...

6

go: shopping
In the afternoon ...

7

talk to: neighbour
Then ...

8

help with: homework
In the evening ...

7 Ask your friend what he loves, likes, hates

Now look at Peter.
He likes ice-cream.

Look at Kitty's face.
She hates ice-cream.

And look at David's face.
He loves ice-cream.

a) Look at the pictures and ask your neighbour.

Example:

You: Do you like dogs? *Your friend:* Yes, I do.

You: Do you like dogs? *Your friend:* No, I don't. I hate dogs.

Find the questions here!

And here you can find the answers.

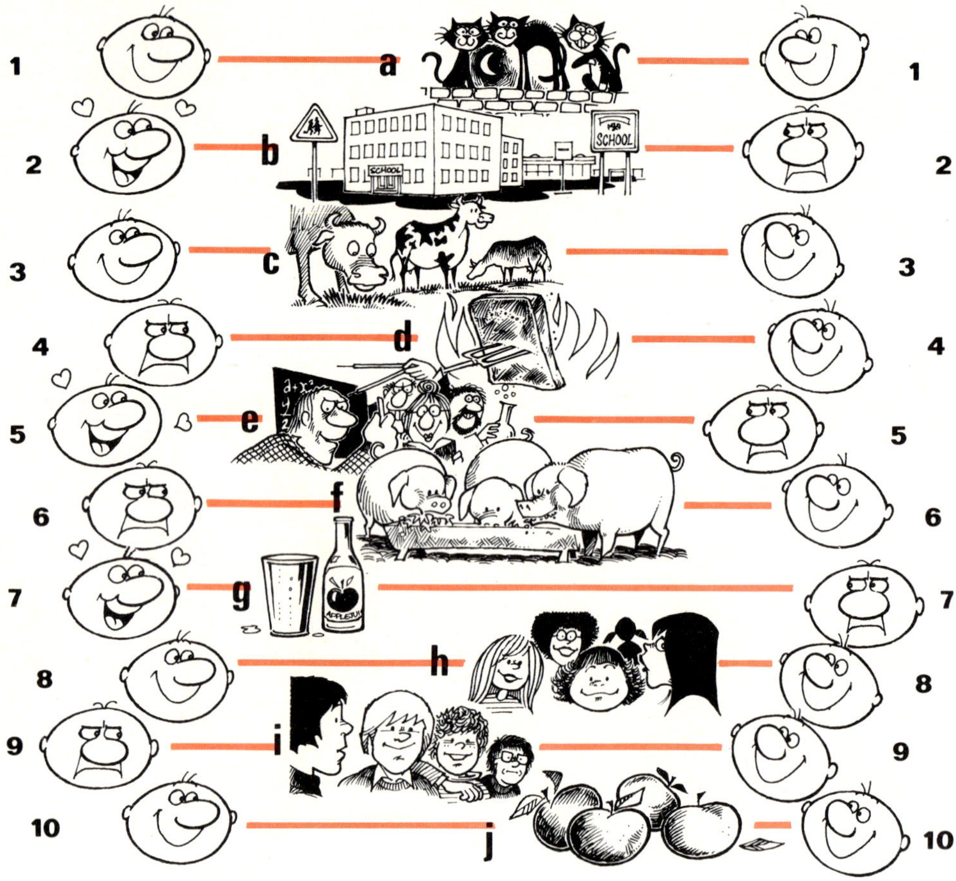

b) Play the juke box.

Example:

You: "4 — c — 7. Tom and Peter."
Tom: Do you hate cows? *(2 = hate, c = cows)*
Peter: Yes, I do. *(7 = hate)*

Now Peter has to call two names and says 6 — a — 10.

c) Say what these boys and girls love, like or hate.

Example: Kitty 2 d
Kitty loves toast.

8 George, the reporter

George ist Reporter einer englischen Schülerzeitung. Daher befragt er den deutschen Austauschschüler Carsten. Die Fragen von George sind in der Redaktion der Schülerzeitung nicht mehr aufzufinden. Carstens Antworten sind jedoch noch vorhanden. Kannst du Georges Fragen herausfinden?

George: . . . ?
Carsten: Yes, I do. I learn English at school.
George: . . . ?
Carsten: Yes, I like London very much.
George: . . . ?
Carsten: Oh no, I hate English school uniforms.
George: . . . ?
Carsten: Yes, I do. I drink tea every morning.
George: . . . ?
Carsten: Yes, we do. We get a lot of homework in Germany.
George: . . . ?
Carsten: No, I don't. We don't learn French at school.
George: . . . ?
Carsten: Oh no, my father says: "Don't drink whisky."
George: . . . ?
Carsten: Yes, I do. I watch TV every night.

9 A game

I pack my suitcase.

a) *Tom:* I pack my suitcase and put a coach in it.
David: I pack my suitcase and put a coach and a ticket-collector in it.
Susan: I pack my suitcase and put a coach and a ticket and a . . .
Claus: DONKEY, DONKEY, DONKEY!!! *(Esel)*

b) Now pack your **clothes** for your holidays.

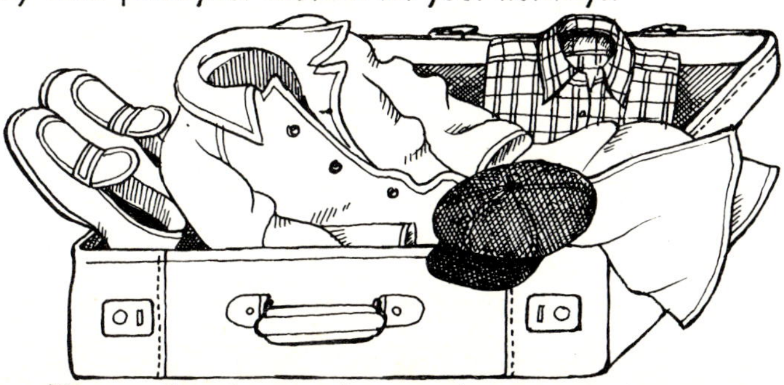

Tom: I pack my suitcase and put a coat in it.
David: . . .

Vocabulary Definitions

a

I am going by . . . from Hamburg to Harwich.	Ich fahre mit dem **Schiff** von Hamburg nach Harwich.	[bəut]	*boat*
Harwich is a town on the . . . of England.	Harwich ist eine Stadt an der englischen **Küste**.	[kəust]	**coast**
The Hamburg children want to . . . their English friends.	Die Kinder aus Hamburg wollen ihre englischen Freunde **besuchen**.	[ˈvizit]	**visit** (to visit)
They often write letters to their . . .	Sie schreiben oft (Briefe) an ihre **Brieffreunde**.	[ˈpenfrendz]	**pen-friends**
		[ˈwustə]	**Worcester**
I want to have a picture of you. Can I . . . of you?	Ich möchte ein Bild von dir haben. Darf ich dich **fotografieren**?	[teik‿ə fˈəutəgrɑ:f]	**take a photograph** (to take)
There are eight boys in the . . . from Hamburg.	Es sind acht Jungen in der **Gruppe** aus Hamburg.	[gru:p]	*group*

b

Sorry. My English isn't very good. I don't . . .	Tut mir leid. Ich kann nicht sehr gut Englisch. Ich **verstehe** das nicht.	[ʌndəˈstænd]	**understand** (to understand)
He does not understand. His English is not very good . . .	Sein Englisch ist **noch nicht** sehr gut.	[jet]	**yet**
Can you say that again? Please . . . that.	Kannst du das noch einmal sagen? **Wiederhole** es bitte.	[riˈpi:t]	**repeat** (to repeat)
Do you understand? Yes, . . .	Hast du es verstanden? — **Ja, ich glaube**.	[aiˈθiŋk səu]	**I think so.**

c

I'm taking three dresses to England. Put them in my . . .	Ich nehme drei Kleider mit nach England. Lege sie bitte in meinen **Koffer**.	[ˈsju:tkeis]	**suitcase**
We must wait for the train on . . .1.	Wir müssen auf den Zug auf **Bahnsteig** 1 warten.	[ˈplætfɔ:m]	**platform**
The train from Harwich to London is the . . .	Der **Zug** von Harwich nach London ist der Anschlußzug von der Fähre.	[ˈbəuttrein] [ˈhæridʒ]	**boat-train** **Harwich**
The . . . can take your suitcases to the train.	Der **Gepäckträger** kann deine Koffer zum Zug bringen.	[ˈpɔ:tə]	**porter**
I have a . . . on the train. I can sit down there.	Ich habe einen reservierten **Platz** im Zug. Da kann ich sitzen.	[si:t]	**seat**
The boat-train has ten . . . My seat is in . . . H.	Der Anschlußzug hat zehn **Wagen**. Mein reservierter Platz ist in **Wagen** H.	[kəutʃ] [kəutʃiz]	*coaches* *coach*
We can have breakfast on the train. There is a . . .	Wir können im Zug frühstücken. Er hat einen **Speisewagen**.	[ˈdainiŋ-kɑ:]	*dining-car*
The waiter has to . . . breakfast. He brings it to the children.	Der Kellner muß das Frühstück **servieren**. Er bringt es den Kindern.	[sə:v]	**serve** (to serve)

d

An orange is a fruit. We often have . . . for breakfast.	Wir trinken oft **Obstsaft** zum Frühstück.	[fru:t dʒu:s]	**fruit juice**

e

Gisela hasn't got her money. So she is . . .	Gisela hat ihr Geld nicht bei sich. Deshalb **weint** sie.	[kraiiŋ]	**crying** (to cry)
Gisela has her money in her . . .	Gisela hat ihr Geld in ihrer **Brieftasche**.	['wɔlit]	**wallet**
Her father gives her some . . . every week.	Ihr Vater gibt ihr ein festes **Taschengeld** jede Woche.	['pɔkitmʌni]	**pocket-money**
The man in the . . . can tell you the right platform.	Der Mann in der **Auskunft** kann dir den richtigen Bahnsteig nennen.	[in'kwaiəri-'ɔfis]	*enquiry office*
You want to know about English money. So you . . . it.	Du möchtest über englisches Geld Bescheid wissen. Dann **frag** doch **danach**.	['ɑ:sk ə'baut]	**ask about** (to ask about)
What is your problem? Tell me. Tell me. . . . it . . . me, please.	Was hast du für ein Problem? Sag es doch. **Erklär** es mir bitte.	[iks'plein tu]	**explain to** (to explain to)
You find something on the platform. What do you do? You go to the . . .	Du findest etwas auf dem Bahnsteig. Was machst du? Du gehst zum **Fundbüro**.	[lɔst 'prɔpəti ɔfis]	**Lost Property Office**
Have you got all your things? Have you got . . .?	Hast du alle deine Sachen? Hast du **alles**?	['evriθiŋ]	**everything**
A man or a woman in an office is a . . .	Ein Mann oder eine Frau in einem Büro ist ein(e) **Beamter/Beamtin** oder ein(e) **Büroangestellte(r)**.	[klɑ:k]	**clerk**
The . . . wants to look at your ticket.	Der **Schaffner** möchte deine Fahrkarte sehen.	['tikit-kəl'ektə]	*ticket-collector*
Everything is OK now. So Gisela is . . .	Jetzt ist alles in Ordnung, Gisela ist **zufrieden**.	['hæpi]	**happy**
A German in London finds English very . . .	Ein Deutscher in London findet Englisch sehr **nützlich**.	['ju:sful]	**useful**
How good is Carsten's English? What's his English . . .?	**Wie** gut ist Carstens Englisch? Wie ist sein Englisch?	[laik]	**like**

Is that the English coast?

Unit 2

a At the youth hostel in London

Frau Schmidt: Good evening, warden.
Warden: Good evening, madam.
Tell me, how long does your group want to stay?
Frau Schmidt: For three nights, please.
Does this hostel serve meals?
Warden: Yes, it does. We can serve you an English breakfast, dinner, then tea, or a late supper.
Frau Schmidt: What does that mean — a late supper? Meat and potatoes?
Warden: No, it doesn't. It means egg on toast, not a big meal. Dinner is at one o'clock. Tea is at six.

Questions

1 Who does Frau Schmidt talk to?
2 How long does the group want to stay?
3 Does the youth hostel serve meals?
4 What meals does it serve?
5 What does a late supper mean?
6 At what time is dinner? And tea?

At the hotel desk

Can you complete this?

Clerk:	Good afternoon, sir. Can I help you?
Mr Mannings:	Good afternoon. I need two rooms for my family.
Clerk:	How long does your family want to stay?
Mr Mannings:	For two nights please. Does this hotel ... meals?
Clerk:	Of course it does. We ... all meals: ... is at 8 o'clock. ... is at half past 12. We serve ... at 5 o'clock or you can have a late ... at half past 8.

b These tourists!

Tourist:	Können Sie mich bitte ...
Taxi-driver:	Sorry, sir, I don't speak German. Don't you speak English?
Tourist:	Es tut mir leid, aber ...
Taxi driver:	No, you don't speak English. I can hear that. Does your friend speak English? No, I can see he doesn't. But perhaps that man over there speaks German? I can ask him. Excuse me, do you speak German, sir?
Man:	No, I don't. All these foreigners in London ...
Taxi-driver:	I like them, and they like us. Don't you agree? Listen to me, sir: Hotel? Hotel?
Tourist:	No, no, no hotel.
Taxi-driver:	Station?
Tourist:	Ja, yes, Paddington Station, ja?
Taxi-driver:	OK, ja. I don't know. Why don't they teach them English over there?

Questions

1 Does the taxi-driver speak German?
2 Does the tourist speak English?
3 Does the man like foreigners?
4 Does the taxi-driver like foreigners?
5 Do you like foreigners?
6 Does the tourist want to go to a hotel?
7 Does the tourist want to go to the station?

The taxi-driver doesn't speak German!

Partner work

You are a German tourist in London. Your English is not very good. Your partner is a Londoner. Ask him if he can speak German.

Frage deinen Partner, ob er Deutsch sprechen kann. Der Partner antwortet, daß er kein Deutsch sprechen kann. Frage ihn dann, ob er weiß, wo das Burton Hotel ist.

You: Excuse me, sir, ...
Partner: No, I ...
You: Do you know ...
Partner: Yes, ... Go to Bingham Street and then left, left again and then...
You: Nicht so schnell, bitte. Not ..., please. Mein Englisch ist nicht sehr gut. My ...
Partner: Come with me. I've got my car here. OK?
You: ... Vielen Dank. Das ist prima. ...
Partner: Good. Follow me, please.

She wants to know everything

Mrs Miller: Waiter, that must be a foreigner at that table. Does he speak French?
Waiter: No, he doesn't.
Mrs Miller: Does he speak German?
Waiter: No, he doesn't.
Mrs Miller: Does he speak Spanish?
Waiter: No, he doesn't.
Mrs Miller: Does he speak English?
Waiter: Yes, he does. He's the manager.

Now act this scene.

C The department store

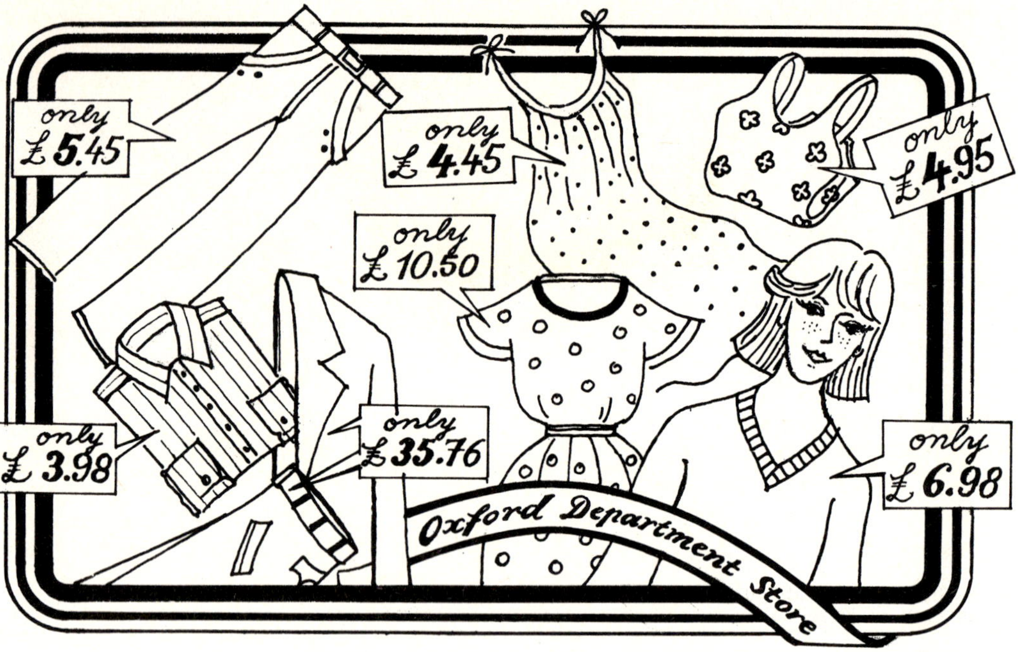

Eine Verkäuferin muß die Gegenstände des Sonderangebots alphabetisch ordnen und aufschreiben. Hinter die Artikel sollen jeweils die Preise aufgeschrieben werden. Diese Liste erhalten alle Kassiererinnen. Stelle die Liste der Verkäuferin zusammen.

d In Oxford Street

Helga, Inge, Carsten and Klaus are now in a big department store in Oxford Street. They are all from the same school in Hamburg, and they are all 14. Helga has black hair. She is quite tall. She always wears a yellow pullover and blue jeans, and she is wearing them today, too. Inge has fair hair and is wearing a blue skirt and a green pullover. Carsten is fair like Inge. He thinks Helga is wonderful.

The boys first go and choose some shirts. The girls go and look at the summer dresses.

Twenty minutes later, they are all in the restaurant. Inge has got a parcel with a swimsuit, and Carsten has got a parcel, too.

"What's in that parcel, Carsten?" Helga asks him.
"It's only a shirt," he tells her, and opens it.
And then the girls laugh. Carsten has got a yellow nightdress in his parcel.
"It's ... em ... it's ... the wrong parcel," Carsten explains to them.
"Does he always wear yellow nightdresses?" Helga asks Inge.
Then a very fat woman comes to their table. She has a blue shirt in her hand and she says to them, "What's that boy doing with my parcel? Give me my parcel, you...!"
She is very cross.
"I'm sorry," says Carsten; now he is laughing, too.

Questions

1 Where are Helga, Inge, Carsten and Klaus?
2 What colour is Helga's hair?
3 And what colour is Inge's hair?
4 Where are they all twenty minutes later?
5 What has Carsten got in his hand?
6 Why do the girls laugh?
7 What is the woman like?
8 Is the woman happy?

Grammar Practice

1 A do – does; don't – doesn't

a) **Does** the **lady** want to go to the station? Yes, **she** does.

b) **Does** the man like tourists? No, **he** doesn't.

1 B

I We You They	**don't**	like toast. want coffee. speak German. understand.

Do	you they	like toast? want coffee? speak German? understand?

He The taxi-driver She Mrs Cooper	**doesn't**	want chips. like tourists. speak English. like England.

Does	he the taxi-driver she Mrs Cooper	want chips? like tourists? speak English? like England?

do + not → don't **does + not → doesn't**

1 C 'do/don't' or 'does/doesn't'?

... **you** all want coffee? Yes, **we** ...
... **he** like English breakfasts? No, **he** ...
... **you** want toast? Yes, **I** ...
... your **friend** speak English? No, **he** ...
... **they** like toast? No, **they** ...
... **she** understand? Yes, **she** ...

2 A I – me; you – you; he – him; she – her; we – us; they – them

a) "**I** can see **him**. But **he** can't see **me**."

b) "Do **you** like **them**?" "No, but **they** like **us**."

c) "Listen to **him**. What does he explain to **them**?"

2 B

I	can see you.	But you can't see	**me.**
You	can see me.	But I can't see	**you.**
He	can see me.	But I can't see	**him.**
She	can see him.	But he can't see	**her.**
It	can see you.	But you can't see	**it.**
We	can see her.	But she can't see	**us.**
They	can see him.	But he can't see	**them.**

2 C

They (Carsten and Klaus) are from the same school. ... (Helga) is a tall girl. She wears ... (a pullover and jeans). ... (Carsten) likes ... (Helga).
"What's that?" ... (Helga) asks ... (Carsten). "It's a shirt," Carsten says to ... (Helga) and opens ... (the parcel). ... (A woman) comes to ... (Carsten and Helga). ... (Carsten and Helga) are laughing.

Exercises

1 Does a tourist often ask silly questions?

Ask your neighbour:

Answer: Yes, he does.
No, he doesn't.

	teacher		drive on the lawn?
	taxi driver		buy a new nightdress?
Does a	waiter	often	wait in the street?
	youth hostel warden		shout "stop it"?
	reporter		ask silly questions?
	tourist		forget his English book?
	pupil		help tourists?
			serve the dinner?
			take photographs?

2 What they like

a) Tom is an awful boy. He hates everything.

The girls close their books now and ask the boys.

Example:

Teacher:	long socks
Girl:	Does Tom hate long socks?
Your friend:	Yes, he does. He hates them.
Teacher:	apples
Girl:	Does he hate apples?
Your friend:	No, he doesn't. He likes them.

b) This is what Betty likes.

You ask a friend in your class: "Does Betty like books?" Books are not in the list, so your friend answers: No, she doesn't. She doesn't like them."
Now all the boys close their books and ask questions about Betty. "Does Betty like..."? The girls answer "Yes, she does" when it's in the list.

3 Tom's family and his friends

Does Tom like his family?

Example:

Does Tom like his grandmother?
No, he doesn't.

3 HDYD CS 2 Textbook 42920

4 What does a waiter do?

a) Look at the pictures and ask questions.

Example:

waiter

to serve people in a restaurant

You: Does a waiter serve people in a restaurant?
Your partner: Yes, he does.

pupil on bike

cycle to school

policeman

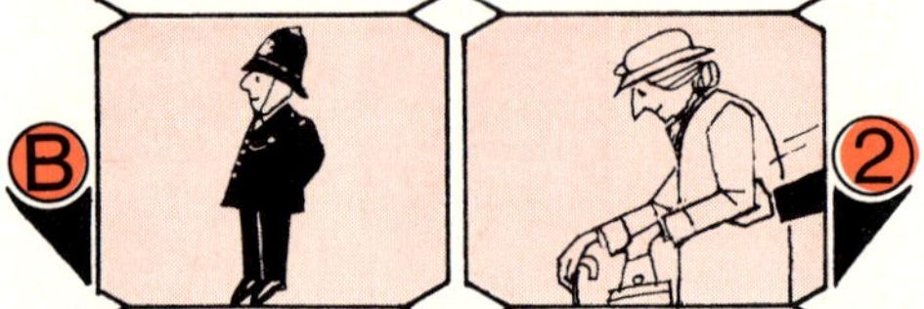

help an old lady

reporter

ask questions

tourist

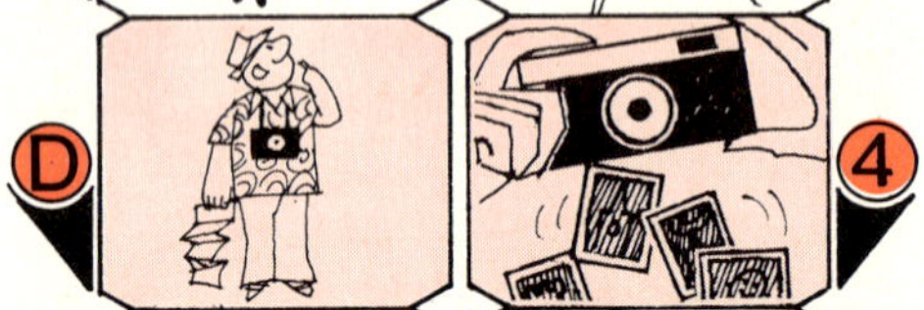

take a lot of photographs

a cook

cook meals

a porter

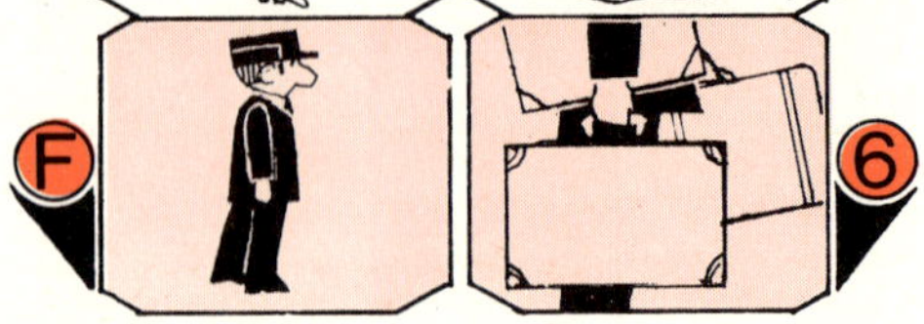

carry suitcases

b) Now you play the juke box!

Say "A — 6" and your friend has to ask: "Does a pupil carry big suitcases?" Someone else answers: "No, he doesn't."

Spielt wieder Musikautomat! Sage z. B. "A — 6" und rufe jemanden auf. Dieser Klassenkamerad stellt die Frage: "Does a pupil carry suitcases?" und ruft einen weiteren Mitschüler auf, der die Antwort geben muß: "No, he doesn't."

c) Now ask your neighbour what these people often do.

Example:

Ask: What does a waiter often do?
Answer: A waiter **serves** people in a restaurant.

5 Father's day

have breakfast

go to work

have tea in the office

write a letter

eat two sandwiches

talk with the manager

go home

read a newspaper

watch TV

Ask questions

a) What does father do at ...?
b) When does he ...?
c) Where does he ...?

Now tell it in a story.

Example: Every morning father has breakfast at 8 o'clock. Then he goes ... After that ... At ... o'clock ...

6 Every morning

Here is what Linda Brown does every morning.
Fill in the right form of the verb.

Every day at 7 o'clock Linda Brown **gets** up. She (have got) ... a lot of things to do. She (wake) ... her husband and (make) ... breakfast. She (eat) ... egg and toast and (drink) ... good hot tea with milk. Mr Brown (eat) ... cornflakes and (drink) ... a cup of coffee. Then Linda (carry) ... the cups and plates into the kitchen.
After breakfast Linda Brown (hurry) ... to Horrid's, the big department store in Station Street. The store (open) ... at 9 o'clock. Linda Brown (wear) ... a white blouse and a grey skirt. She (be) ... a shop assistant at Horrid's. All the other shop assistants (wear) ... white blouses and grey skirts, too.

7 Tim and Tom

a) Tim und Tom sind Zwillingsbrüder. Und trotzdem haben sie einen ganz unterschiedlichen Geschmack. Schau dir ihre Gesichter an und finde heraus, was sie mögen oder nicht mögen. Sei vorsichtig mit "it" und "them".

Example:

You: Does Tim like eggs?
Your friend: Yes, he does, but Tom doesn't like them.

b) Oh, these children!

Their mother is talking about her sons to her neighbour. Here is what she says:

Tim likes clean shoes, but Tom doesn't like them.
Tom wants a late supper, but Tim doesn't want it.
Tom likes Maths lessons, but Tim ...
Tim likes marmalade, but Tom ...
Tom likes Peter, but Tim ...
Tim likes Susan, but Tom ...
Tom likes Hazel, but Tim ...
Tom likes his father, but Tim ...
Tom likes me, but Tim ...

8 What do you ...? When do you ...? Where do you ...? Why do you ...?

A long list of answers. Can you find the questions?

1 No, my father hasn't got a taxi.
2 No, teachers don't serve meals.
3 Yes, reporters ask questions.
4 Yes, I like ice-cream.
5 No, I don't hate beer.
6 Yes, the policeman stands in the street.
7 I'm fine.
8 I'm ... years old.
9 I live in ...
10 This ice-cream is 15p.
11 Yes, I like the Beatles.
12 Yes, I speak English.
13 No, my father isn't a policeman.
14 No, my bike isn't black, it's blue.
15 No, we haven't got a dog.
16 No, policemen don't cycle in the school garden.
17 No, the headmaster doesn't clean our school.
18 No, the ticket collector doesn't write tests.
19 No, teachers don't ask silly questions.
20 I have breakfast in the kitchen, not in the dining-room.

9 Find more words

Find more words to fit these generic terms?

Finde weitere Wörter zu den Oberbegriffen.

a) teacher, ... (jobs)
b) banana, ... (fruit)
c) coffee, ... (drinks)
d) breakfast, ... (meals)
e) kitchen, ... (rooms in the house)
f) jeans, ... (clothes)

10 Word games

a) Can you find the next words?

Versuche Wörter zu finden, die mit dem letzten Buchstaben des vorhergehenden Wortes beginnen.

```
honestly
    e
    sister
         a
         d
         i
         omelette
                a
                test
                   .
                   .
                   . . . . .
```

b) Here is a long word. Find a new word for each letter.

Hier ist ein langes Wort. Findet weitere Wörter, die mit den einzelnen Buchstaben dieses Wortes beginnen.

```
chalk
o ...
n ...
v ...
e ...
r ...
s ...
a ...
t ...
i ...
o ...
n ...
```

Vocabulary Definitions

a

Teenagers often don't stay at hotels but at the cheaper ...	Jugendliche übernachten oft nicht in Hotels, sondern in den billigeren **Jugendherbergen**.	[ˈjuːθ hɔstəl]	*youth hostels*
The boss or manager of the youth hostel is the ...	Der Leiter einer Jugendherberge ist der **Herbergsvater**.	[ˈwɔːdən]	**warden**
How ... does your group want to stay?	Wie **lange** möchte eure Gruppe bleiben?	[lɔŋ]	**long**
Breakfast, dinner and supper are ...	Frühstück, Mittag-, Abendessen sind **Mahlzeiten**.	[miːlz]	**meals**
We have tea at six and then a late ...,	Wir essen um sechs **Abendbrot** und dann noch ein spätes Abendessen*.	[ˈsʌpə]	**supper**
I don't understand: what does the word Struwwelpeter ...?	Ich verstehe das nicht: was **heißt** (das Wort) Struwwelpeter?	[miːn]	**mean** (to mean)

* Die englischen **Mahlzeiten** können im Vergleich zu deutschen ganz Unterschiedliches bedeuten: **lunch'** ist meist ein leichtes Mittagessen; **'dinner'** ist Mittag, wenn es die Hauptmahlzeit ist, abends ist es ein warmes Essen. **'Tea'** ist oft eine warme Mahlzeit, nicht mit ‚Kaffeetrinken' zu verwechseln, eher ein Abendbrot; **'supper'** ist ein später Imbiß.

b

I don't ... French, but I ... English.	Ich spreche kein Französisch, aber ich **spreche** Englisch.	[spi:k]	**speak** (to speak)
Please say that again. I can't ... you.	Sag das bitte noch einmal. Ich kann dich nicht **hören**.	[ˈhiə]	**hear** (to hear)
A German in London is a ...	Ein Deutscher in London ist ein **Fremder/Ausländer**.	[ˈfɔrinə]	**foreigner**
Don't you think so, too? Don't you ...?	Findest du das nicht auch? Bist du nicht **der gleichen Meinung**?	[əˈgri:]	**agree** (to agree)
Our English teacher ... English.	Unser Englisch**lehrer unterrichtet** Englisch.	[ti:tʃə] [ti:tʃiz]	**teacher** **teaches** (to teach)

c

The very big shops, the ..., are in Oxford Street.	Die ganz großen Läden, die **Kaufhäuser**, sind in der Oxford Street.	[diˈpa:tmənt stɔ:z]	**department stores**
In August, in ..., girls wear ... dresses.	Im August, im **Sommer**, tragen die Mädchen Sommerkleider.	[ˈsʌmə]	**summer**
Look! She is in the water now and she is wearing her new ...	Guck mal, sie ist jetzt im Wasser und hat ihren neuen **Badeanzug** an.	[ˈswimsju:t]	**swimsuit**
Helga always wears blue ...	Helga trägt immer **Bluejeans**.	[dʒi:nz]	*jeans*
Carsten has got a yellow ... in his parcel.	Carsten hat ein gelbes **Nachthemd** in seinem Paket.	[ˈnaitdres]	**nightdress**
Inge is not wearing jeans but a blue ...	Inge trägt keine Jeans, sondern einen blauen **Rock**.	[skə:t]	**skirt**
It is cold today. So Inge is wearing a green ...	Heute ist es kalt. Deshalb hat Inge einen grünen **Pullover** an.	[ˈpuləuvə]	*pullover*

d

The boys and girls are ... from Hamburg.	Die Jungen und Mädchen sind **alle** aus Hamburg.	[ɔ:l]	**all**
They are all from one school. They are all from the ... school.	Sie sind alle von einer Schule. Sie sind alle von **derselben** Schule.	[seim]	**same**
Helga has black ...	Helga hat schwarzes **Haar**.	[hɛə]	**hair**
Helga is not small. She is ...	Helga ist nicht klein. Sie ist **groß (lang)**.	[tɔ:l]	**tall**
She is not very tall. She is ... tall.	Sie ist nicht sehr groß. Sie ist **ziemlich** groß.	[kwait]	**quite**
She has not got black hair. She is ...	Sie hat kein schwarzes Haar. Sie ist **blond**.	[fɛə]	**fair**
Carsten is fair ... Inge.	Carsten ist blond **wie** Inge.	[laik]	**like**
The boys look at the shirts and then ... two.	Die Jungen begucken sich die Oberhemden und **nehmen (wählen)** dann zwei davon.	[tʃu:z]	**choose** (to choose)
Inge has got a swimsuit in her ...	Inge hat einen Badeanzug in ihrem **Paket**.	[ˈpa:səl]	**parcel**
Carsten opens his parcel and the girls ...	Carsten macht sein Paket auf, und die Mädchen **lachen**.	[la:f]	**laugh** (to laugh)
This woman eats too much cake. So she is too ...	Die Frau ißt zuviel Kuchen. Sie ist zu **dick**.	[fæt]	**fat**
Carsten has got the woman's parcel. So she is very ...	Carsten hat das Paket der Frau. Deshalb ist sie sehr **ärgerlich**.	[krɔs]	**cross**

Unit 3

a On Worcester station

David: Who is your partner, Eileen?
Eileen: Her name is Ingrid. Look, here's her photograph.
David: Wow! She looks great. Is she older than you?
Eileen: No, she isn't. She is as old as I am. What about your partner?
David: He is younger than I am, but he looks older. Here's his photograph.
Eileen: Oh, he looks very nice. What's his name?
David: It's Carsten, Carsten Schröder.
Eileen: Oh, look, there's the London train. It's earlier than usual.

Questions

1 Who is Ingrid?
2 What does she look like?
3 Is Eileen older than Ingrid?
4 Who is Carsten?
5 Is Carsten older than David?
6 Is the London train late?

Elsie looks great!

David is looking at a photograph of Eileen and her friends. All of them are as old as Eileen. Here is what they say:

Example:

David: Elsie looks great. Is she older than you?
Eileen: No, she isn't. She is as old as I am.

Go on with: Kitty, Tina, Belinda, Susan, Mary

b Welcome to Worcester

1 Eileen is running **towards** her friend Ingrid.

2 David Moss is **rushing** towards Carsten.

3 Carsten is **smiling**. He is very **glad** he is in Worcester.

4 Ingrid is getting a big **kiss** from Eileen's mother now.

5 David's father and Carsten are **shaking hands** now.

6 The headmaster of the Worcester school is **welcoming** Frau Schmidt.

Questions

1 Where is Eileen running?
2 What is David Moss doing?
3 Why is Carsten smiling?
4 Who gives Ingrid a big kiss?
5 What is David's father doing?
6 What is the headmaster doing?

At Worcester station

Can you complete this?

Ingrid is running ... Eileen. Carsten is ... towards David. David is ... Carsten is carrying a ... They are on ... 10. David's father and Eileen's mother are ... hands. The dining-car is ... A ... is carrying two suitcases. The ... is looking at the tickets.

C The Moss family

1 *David:* Mum, this is Carsten. Carsten, meet my mother.

2 *Mrs Moss:* Hello, Carsten. We're glad you're here at last.

3 *David:* Meet my sister Wendy, Carsten. She's a year younger than I am.

4 *Carsten:* I don't believe it. She's as tall as you are.
Wendy: Thank you, Carsten.

5 *Mrs Moss:* Come along, Carsten. My car is outside.

6 *Wendy:* Look, Carsten, that's our cathedral over there.

7 And on the right you can see the River Severn.

8 *Carsten:* Worcester looks lovely.
Mrs Moss: Yes, it's nice, but Hamburg is much bigger, of course.

Questions

1 Who does Carsten meet?
2 What does Mrs Moss say to Carsten?
3 How old is David's sister?
4 How tall is Wendy?
5 Where is Mr Moss's car?
6 What does Wendy show Carsten first?
7 What can Carsten see on the right?
8 Is Worcester as big as Hamburg?

d In the taxi

Driver: Where to, sir?
Herr Henning: 22, Keats Avenue, please. Is that far?
Driver: It can't be much nearer, sir. It's only a mile from here. Are you just here for the weekend, sir?
Herr Henning: No, I'm staying longer than that.
Driver: Well, here we are, sir, number 22.
Herr Henning: How much is it?
Driver: Just £1, sir.
Herr Henning: Oh, I've only got a ten-pound note.
Driver: You haven't got anything smaller than that, sir?
Herr Henning: Yes, I think I've got two 50p pieces. Ah, yes, here you are. And these two 10p pieces are for you.
Driver: Thank you very much, sir. Have a nice holiday.

Questions

1 Where does Herr Henning want to go to?
2 How far is it?
3 Is Herr Henning staying in Worcester just for the weekend?
4 How much does the driver want?
5 Has Herr Henning got anything smaller than a ten-pound-note?
6 How many 10p pieces does Herr Henning give the driver?
7 What does the driver say to Herrn Henning?

Grammar Practice

1 A . . . younger than . . . / . . . as old as . . .

Tim is **taller than** Tony.

Tom is **as tall as** Tim.

'Haven't you got **anything nicer**?"
"Yes, that's **much nicer.**"

1 B taller, earlier . . .

Beachte die Schreibweise!

young + er → younger		
old + er → older		
tall + er → taller		
small + er → smaller		
cheap + er → cheaper		
early + er → earlier	y → i	
silly + er → sillier		
busy + er → busier		
pretty + er → prettier		
nice + er → nicer	— e + er	
safe + er → safer		
fat + er → fatter	+ t	+ er
hot + er → hotter		
big + er → bigger	+ g	

1 C -er or not?

Beachte die Wörter 'than', 'as . . . as', 'anything', 'much'.

a) This is my sister Wendy. She's a year (young) . . . than I am. So I am (old) . . . than my sister. But Wendy is as (tall) . . . as I am.
b) Hamburg is (big) . . . than Worcester, but London is (big) . . . than Hamburg.
c) "How much is the newspaper?" "8p. Oh, haven't you got anything (small) . . . than that?" "Yes, I think, I've got a 10p piece. "That's much (nice) . . ."

Exercises

1 Meet my friends

Tim Baker, 11; Tom Cartwright, 12; Brenda Lee, 13; Joan White, 14; Susan Brown, 10.

a) Ask your partner:

b) Now ask your partner:

Go on with: Brenda, Tom, Joan, Susan

2 Is Green's cheaper than Brown's?

R a) What can you get for £2?
For £2 you can get ...
Now go on with £3, £5, £7, ...

b) How much are the skirts at Brown's/Green's?
At Brown's/Green's they are ...

c) Are the summer dresses at Brown's cheaper than at Green's?
The summer dresses are cheaper at Green's.

d) You are standing in front of Brown's shop window, and your friend is standing in front of Green's shop window. Which shop is cheaper?

Example:

You:	Oh, look they sell cheap skirts at Brown's. Do they also sell skirts at Green's?
Your friend:	Yes, they do.
You:	How much are the skirts at Green's?
Your friend:	They are £5.85.
You:	Oh, I see, the skirts are cheaper at Green's.

Go on and ask about the pullovers, dresses, swimsuits, jeans, nightdresses.

e) Draw the two shop windows on the board and act this scene.

3 Teenagers

a) Who is smaller, taller, older, younger?

Jim 15 Tom 13 Susan 14 Hazel 12 Brenda 16.

Jim is older than Tom
but Tom is taller than Jim.
Tom is younger than Susan
but Brenda is smaller than Tom,
and Susan is ...
but Hazel is ...

b) Ask questions about these teenagers:

Example:
Who is taller, Tom or Susan?
Susan is taller than Tom.

Go on. Compare the other boys and girls, too.

c) Now talk to your neighbour:

4 When do they get up?

Mr Baker | Mum | Mr Roberts | Mrs Barber | Mr Brown

a) Ask your partner:

Go on with Mum, Mr Roberts, Mrs Barber and Mr Brown.

b) Ask your partner:

Example:

You: Who gets up earlier/later, Mr Baker or Mum?
Your friend: Mr Baker gets up at 5 o'clock, but Mum gets up at a quarter past six. So Mr Baker gets up earlier than Mum.

Go on with Mrs Barber and Mum, Mr Baker and Mr Roberts, Mr Roberts and Mum, Mr Baker and Mr Brown ...

4 HDYD CS 2 Textbook 42920

5 David's and Eileen's friends ■

David and Eileen are talking about their friends. Here is what they say.

> *Example:*
>
> *David:* Look, this is Peter's photograph.
> *Eileen:* Is he older than you?
> *David:* No, he isn't. He is as old as I am.
> *Eileen:* Oh, he looks very nice.

Talk to your partner

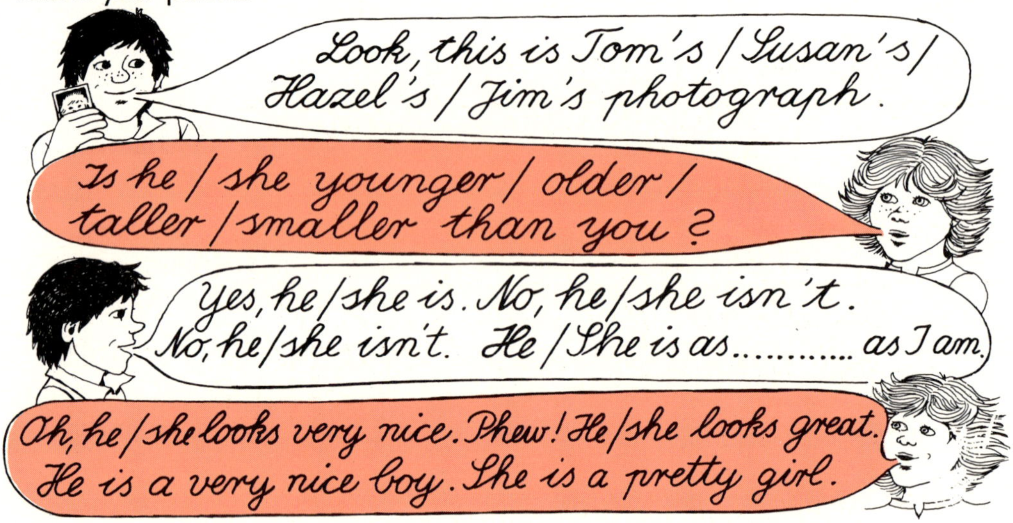

Now you are Eileen and your neighbour is David. Start a conversation.

6 Carsten's second day in England

David, 14, introduces his German friend Carsten, 15, to his friend George, 16. What does George say?

David: Meet my friend Carsten.
George: . . .
Carsten: Hello, George.
George: . . .
Carsten: I'm 15 years old.
George: . . .
Carsten: No, David isn't older than I am. He's only 14.
How old are you?
George: . . .
Carsten: So you are a year older than I am.
George: . . .

Carsten: I live in Hamburg.
George: ...
Carsten: Yes, I like England very much.
George: ...
Carsten: No, my parents don't speak English.
George: ...
Carsten: No, I hate English breakfasts.
David: Come along, George and Carsten. Let's look at Worcester.

7 Ingrid meets Eileen's family

Fill in the correct form of the following verbs:

Setze die richtige Form der folgenden Wörter an der richtigen Stelle ein:

introduce, smile, welcome, rush, shake

a) At Eileen's home. Eileen ... Ingrid to her father and her mother. Then they ... hands. Mr Dent ... and ... Ingrid. He says: "I'm glad you are here. Eileen can show you our house and your room now." Then the two girls ... upstairs.

b) Ingrid likes Eileen's house.

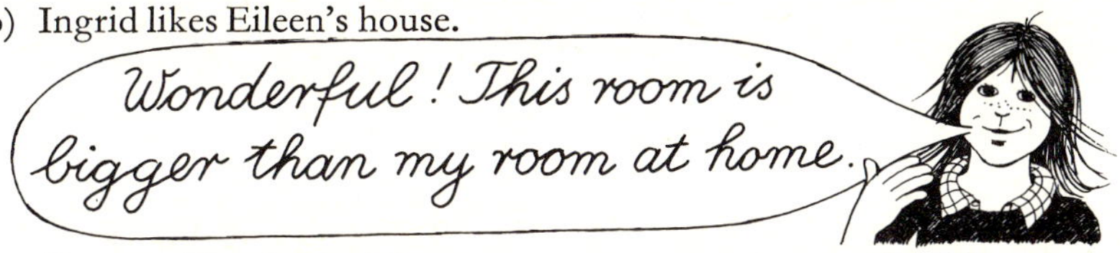

Go on with: house/nice
bike/fast
your mother/happy
this bed/nice
your tape recorder/small
garden/big
your father/young
your father/tall
your TV set/new

8 Older? Younger? Cheaper? Colder? Hotter?

Who is older, younger, taller, smaller? What is hotter, colder, bigger, smaller?

Example:
The shorts are cheaper than the jeans.

(cheap)

(old/young)

(hot/cold)

(early/late)

(tall/small)

(big/small)

9 Peter's day

a) Ask questions about these pictures.

Example:

What does Peter do at . . . o'clock?
When does Peter . . . ?
Where does Peter . . . ?

b) Write the story about Peter's day.

c) Now tell your neighbour when **you** do these things and where you do them.
Your neighbour must ask you: When do you get up?
When do you have breakfast?
. . . ?

10 A game

Which words go together?

Welche Wörter passen zusammen?

Example:

You: pupil
Your friend: teacher, school, pencil . . .

Go on with: pencil, house, cat, bread, tea, table

11 Oh these Howdoyoudolians!

Help! Stop them! Put these words right again.

Hilf dem Schriftsetzer und korrigiere die verdrehten Wörter.

Vocabulary Definitions

a

Isn't Ingrid pretty? Yes, she . . . great!	Ist Ingrid nicht schick (flott, hübsch)? Ja, sie **sieht** toll (großartig) **aus**.	[luks]	**looks** (to look)
Ingrid is older . . . you.	Ingrid ist älter **als** du.	[ðən]	**than**
My partner isn't as old as I am. He is . . .	Mein Partner ist nicht so alt wie ich. Er ist **jünger**.	[jʌŋgə]	**younger** (young)
When does your party start? At eight?	Wann geht deine Party los? Um acht?		
No, . . . than that. At seven.	Nein, **früher**. Um sieben.	[ˈɜːliə]	**earlier** (early)
Look, Jack's already here! Yes, he's earlier than . . .	Guck mal, Jack ist schon hier. Ja, er ist früher da als **sonst immer**.	[ˈjuːʒəl]	**usual**

b

It's nice you are here. . . . to Worcester.	Es ist fein, daß du hier bist. **Willkommen** in Worcester.	[ˈwelkʌm]	**welcome** (to welcome)
You're going too fast. You needn't . . .	Du gehst zu schnell. Du brauchst dich nicht zu **beeilen / so zu rennen**.	[rʌʃ]	**rush** (to rush)
He is rushing . . . him.	Er rennt **auf ihn zu**.	[təˈwɔːdz]	**towards**
Carsten is very happy. He is . . .	Carsten ist sehr zufrieden. Er **lächelt / freut sich**.	[smailiŋ]	**smiling** (to smile)
My mother is OK now. Oh, I'm very	Meiner Mutter geht es wieder gut. Oh, bin ich **glücklich**.	[glæd]	**glad**
Bye-bye, dear. Isn't your old mother getting a . . . today?	Wiedersehen, mein(e) Liebe(r). Na, kriegt deine alte Mutter heute nicht einen **Kuß**.	[kis]	**kiss**
David rushes towards Carsten and then they . . .	David rennt auf Carsten zu, und dann **geben sie sich die Hand**.	[ʃeik ˈhændz]	**shake hands** (to shake hands)

c

Ah, there's my new friend Bill, Mum. Mum, . . . my new friend Bill.	Dies ist mein neuer Freund Bill, Mammi. Mammi, darf ich dir meinen neuen Freund Bill **vorstellen**.	[miːt]	**meet** (to meet)
Where is Tom? Ah, there he is . . . You're very late, Tom!	Wo ist Tom? Ach, da ist er ja **endlich**. Du kommst reichlich spät, Tom.	[ət ˈlɑːst]	**at last**
Wendy is a . . . younger than David.	Wendy ist ein **Jahr** jünger als David.	[jəː]	**year**
You've got £950 in your wallet? I don't . . . it!	Du hast 950 Pfund in deiner Brieftasche? Das **glaube** ich nicht.	[bəˈliːv]	**believe** (to believe)
The car is waiting. . . ., Carsten.	Das Auto wartet. Nun **komm schon**, Carsten.	[kʌm əˈlɔŋ]	**come along** (to come along)
Where's your brother? He's waiting . . . He doesn't want to come in.	Wo ist dein Bruder? Er wartet **draußen**. Er will nicht hereinkommen.	[ˈautˈsaid]	**outside**
Every Sunday morning we go to the . . . in Worcester.	Jeden Sonntag morgen gehen wir in die **Kathedrale** (in den Dom) von Worcester.	[kəˈθiːdrəl]	*cathedral*
The Severn is Worcester's . . .	Die Severn ist der **Fluß** von Worcester.	[ˈrivə]	**river**

d

I want to go to Keat's . . ., please.	Ich möchte bitte zur Keats **Allee**.	[ˈævinjuː]	*Avenue*
How . . . is it from here to Dover?	Wie **weit** ist es von hier nach Dover?	[fɑː]	**far**
Braunschweig is . . . to Berlin than Stuttgart	Braunschweig liegt **näher** zu Berlin als Stuttgart	[ˈniːrə]	**nearer** (near)
It is only one . . . from here to the station.	Es ist nur eine **Meile** (= 1,6 Kilometer) von hier bis zum Bahnhof.	[mail]	*mile*
Come on Saturday and Sunday: come for the . . .	Komm Sonnabend und Sonntag. Komm über's **Wochenende**.	[ˈwiːkənd]	*weekend*
A £10-note? Haven't you got . . . smaller? Yes, I've got two 50p pieces.	Eine 10 Pfund-Note? Haben Sie es nicht **irgendwie** kleiner? Ja, ich habe zwei 50p Stücke.	[ˈeniθiŋ]	**anything**
You're going to Timmendorf? Have a nice . . .!	Sie fahren nach Timmendorf? Schönen **Urlaub**!	[ˈhɔlidei]	**holiday**

Unit 4

a Mrs Moss's calendar

Questions

1 When does Mrs Moss want to have her garden party?
2 Why does she want to telephone Mrs Gibbs?
3 What does she want to do on Tuesday 2nd July?
4 When does she want to buy the beer?
5 What does she want to order from the baker?
6 What does she want to do on Friday?
7 At what time does the garden party begin?

Happy birthday to you!

Can you complete this?

S		S	5th JUNE
M		M	6th JUNE
T		T	7th JUNE
W	1st JUNE	W	8th JUNE
T	2nd JUNE	T	9th JUNE
F	3rd JUNE baker! sausages	F	10th JUNE
S	4th JUNE my birthday party	S	11th JUNE
		S	12th JUNE

a) This is Wendy's . . .

The . . . of her birthday party is . . . On . . . 1st June she writes the . . . cards. On . . . 3rd June she . . . 50 sausages, then she goes to the . . . and . . . three big cakes.

b) Look at the calendar and ask your neighbour.

Go on asking about these dates: 3rd, 5th, 11th, 1st, 7th, 2nd, 8th, . . .

b What can the German guests do?

Secretary: What can our German guests do tomorrow, sir?
Headmaster: I think I'll show them round the school.
Secretary: Will they have dinner at school?
Headmaster: Yes, please order fifteen extra dinners. What's the date tomorrow?
Secretary: It's Tuesday, 13th July. It's sausages on Tuesday.
Headmaster: Ah well, that's OK. The Germans will like our sausages.
Secretary: And after dinner, sir?
Headmaster: The German teacher and I will show them the town. We'll take them to the cathedral, and then, on Wednesday ...

Questions

1 Who will show the German guests round the school?
2 Where will the Germans have their dinner?
3 How many German guests are there?
4 What day is 13th July? A Monday?
5 What will the Germans get for dinner on that day?
6 Where will the headmaster take them after dinner?

What's on for our German quests on Saturday?

this morning	the town
tomorrow	Windsor Castle
on Wednesday	London
on Thursday	our house
on Tuesday	our garden
on Friday	our English restaurant
next year	Oxford

C Monday morning at the Moss family's house

1 Wednesday, 14th July, seven o'clock. Mrs Moss is a **nurse** in a **hospital.** So she has to get up early.

2 Mr Moss gets up early, too, **because** he is a **postman.**

3 Mrs Moss **knocks** at Wendy's door.

4 "Time to get up, Wendy!" she shouts.

5 David, Carsten and Wendy have their breakfast at eight.

6 "Have **another piece of toast**, Carsten," says Wendy.

7 School in England **starts** at nine o'clock. So they have to leave the house at half past eight.

Questions

1 Why does Mrs Moss have to get up early?
2 Why does Mr Moss get up early?
3 What does Mrs Moss always do then?
4 What does she shout?
5 When do David and Carsten have their breakfast?
6 What does Wendy say to Carsten?
7 Why do they have to leave the house at half past eight?

d Renate wants to go home

That Wednesday evening Carsten is having supper with the Moss family.
"Listen, Mum, somebody is knocking at the door," David says, and goes and opens it.
"It's a German girl, Carsten. She's crying and she wants to see you," he shouts into the room.
Carsten goes to the door and sees Renate.
"Bring her into the dining-room, Carsten," shouts Mrs Moss. "Perhaps she'll have a cup of tea with us."
So Carsten takes Renate into the dining-room and introduces her.
"What's the matter, dear? Why are you crying?" Mrs Moss asks.
"I want to go home," Renate explains.
"But why?" Mr Moss asks. "Don't you like your English pen-friend?"

"Yes, she's all right, but her brother Jack is awful, and the food is awful, and it's all so different, and ..."
"I know, dear," says Mrs Moss. "It's difficult for you. But why don't you telephone your mother and talk to her about it?"
"Oh, Mrs Moss, can I? Have you got a telephone? I'll pay, of course, but please dial the number for me. I don't know how to telephone Germany."
Mrs Moss lifts the receiver and dials 192 for Enquiries. "Can you give me the code for Hamburg in Germany, please?" she asks. "Ah, thank you. And how much will that cost for three minutes? Right. Thank you again."
Then she dials the very long number and gives the receiver to Renate.
Three minutes later, Renate is a happy girl again. "Hamburg is quite near, really," she says to Mrs Moss, and smiles.

Questions

1 What is Carsten doing on that Wednesday evening?
2 Why does David go to the door?
3 Why does Carsten go to the door?
4 Why is Renate crying?
5 Why does she want to go home?
6 Who can Renate telephone?
7 Why does Renate ask Mrs Moss to dial the number?
8 How does Mrs Moss get Enquiries?
9 How long does Renate telephone?

Grammar Practice

1 A the first, the second, . . .

Can you complete these numbers in the lift?

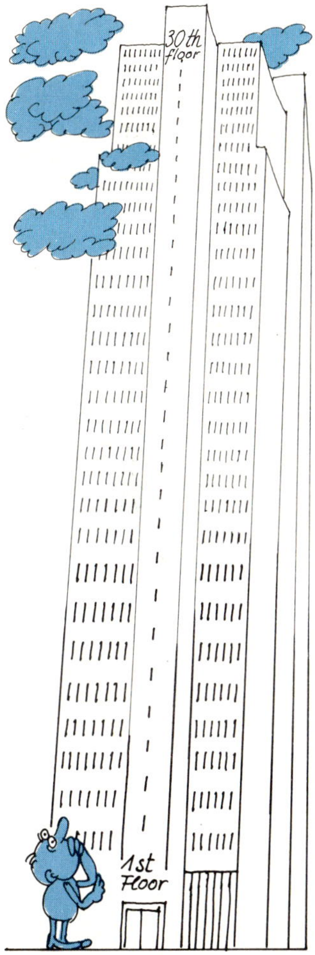

Floor		Floor	
15th	. . .	30th	. . .
14th	. . .	29th	. . .
13th	. . .	28th	. . .
12th	. . .	27th	. . .
11th	. . .	26th	. . .
10th	. . .	25th	twenty-fifth
9th	. . .	24th	twenty-fourth
8th	. . .	23rd	twenty-third
7th	. . .	22nd	twenty-second
6th	. . .	21st	twenty-first
5th	fifth	20th	twentieth
4th	fourth	19th	. . .
3rd	third	18th	. . .
2nd	second	17th	. . .
1st	first	16th	. . .

2 A I'll go by bus

"I can't go by bike, so **I'll go** by bus **tomorrow**."

2 B

I		I'll	go by bike **tomorrow.**
We		We'll	see our friends **next week.**
You	will	→ You'll	buy a record **on Monday.**
They		They'll	go to the party **on Sunday.**
He		He'll	watch football **this afternoon.**
She		She'll	play table-tennis **tomorrow.**

Now ask the questions!

1 **When** will you go by bike?
2 **When** will you see your ...
3 **When** will you ...
4 **When** ...
5 ...
6 ...

Exercises

1 This is the first exercise (1st)

Example:

You: When is your birthday?
Your friend: My birthday is in May.

a) Now you ask your friends. Look at the picture.

Which of these months are in summer or winter? Write a list.

Which of these months is very cold or hot?

Example:

January is very cold.
February ...

b) Now make more sentences like this:

January is the coldest month; and October is colder than July.

...

2 This is the second exercise (2nd)

At Wendy's birthday party

1980

January					
S		6	13	20	27
M		7	14	21	28
T	1	8	15	22	29
W	2	9	16	23	30
T	3	10	17	24	31
F	4	11	18	25	
S	5	12	19	26	

April					
S		6	13	20	27
M		7	14	21	28
T	1	8	15	22	29
W	2	9	16	23	30
T	3	10	17	24	
F	4	11	18	25	
S	5	12	19	26	

July					
S		6	13	20	27
M		7	14	21	28
T	1	8	15	22	29
W	2	9	16	23	30
T	3	10	17	24	31
F	4	11	18	25	
S	5	12	19	26	

October					
S		5	12	19	26
M		6	13	20	27
T		7	14	21	28
W	1	8	15	22	29
T	2	9	16	23	30
F	3	10	17	24	31
S	4	11	18	25	

February					
S		3	10	17	24
M		4	11	18	25
T		5	12	19	26
W		6	13	20	27
T		7	14	21	28
F	1	8	15	22	29
S	2	9	16	23	

May					
S		4	11	18	25
M		5	12	19	26
T		6	13	20	27
W		7	14	21	28
T	1	8	15	22	29
F	2	9	16	23	30
S	3	10	17	24	31

August					
S		3	10	17	24	31
M		4	11	18	25	
T		5	12	19	26	
W		6	13	20	27	
T		7	14	21	28	
F	1	8	15	22	29	
S	2	9	16	23	30	

November					
S		2	9	16	23	30
M		3	10	17	24	
T		4	11	18	25	
W		5	12	19	26	
T		6	13	20	27	
F		7	14	21	28	
S	1	8	15	22	29	

March					
S		2	9	16	23	30
M		3	10	17	24	31
T		4	11	18	25	
W		5	12	19	26	
T		6	13	20	27	
F		7	14	21	28	
S	1	8	15	22	29	

June					
S	1	8	15	22	29
M	2	9	16	23	30
T	3	10	17	24	
W	4	11	18	25	
T	5	12	19	26	
F	6	13	20	27	
S	7	14	21	28	

September					
S		7	14	21	28
M	1	8	15	22	29
T	2	9	16	23	30
W	3	10	17	24	
T	4	11	18	25	
F	5	12	19	26	
S	6	13	20	27	

December					
S		7	14	21	28
M	1	8	15	22	29
T	2	9	16	23	30
W	3	10	17	24	31
T	4	11	18	25	
F	5	12	19	26	
S	6	13	20	27	

The children want to know their friends' birthdays.

In diesem Spiel versuchen die Kinder, mit möglichst wenig Fragen den Geburtstag ihrer Freunde herauszufinden. Den Gewinnern winken viele Preise.

Betty: Is your birthday in winter, George?
George: Yes, it is.
Betty: Is it in February?
George: Yes, it is.
Betty: Is it in the third week of February?
George: No, it isn't.
Betty: Is it in the first week of February?
George: Yes, it is.
Betty: Is it a Wednesday?
George: No, it isn't.
Betty: Is it a Thursday?
George: Yes, it is.
Betty: Then it's Thursday, 7th February!
George: You are right.

Now act this in your class. Look at the calendar in your English books. (Do you know your teacher's birthday?)

3 The third exercise (3rd)

Days and dates

Example:

You: Today is Wednesday.
Your friend: Tomorrow is Thursday.
You: Today is the sixth of June.
Your friend: Tomorrow is the seventh of June.
You: June is the sixth month of the year.
Your friend: The seventh month is July.

Can you complete this?

You: Today is ...
Your friend: Tomorrow is ...
You: Today is ...
Your friend: Tomorrow is ...
You: January is ...
Your friend: The second month is ...

Now talk to your friends. Here are some days and dates.

April — 1 — Sunday
July — 17 — Wednesday
August — 30 — Tuesday
May — 5 — Monday
February — 28 — Thursday

November — 7 — Wednesday
March — 20 — Friday
January — 22 — Sunday
October — 12 — Monday
December — 31 — Saturday

4 This is the fourth exercise (4th)

Write this list:

January 1st is the first day of the year
February 1st is the 32nd day of the year
March 1st ...
...
...
...

5 HDYD CS 2 Textbook 42920

5 This is the fifth exercise (5th)

When is my birthday?

Schau dir die Liste aus Übung 4 und den Kalender aus Übung 2 noch einmal genau an. Jetzt findest du sicher das Datum der Geburtstage leicht heraus.

Example:

You:	My birthday is on the 69th day of the year. What day is it?
Your friend:	Is it 7th March?
You:	No, it isn't. Think again.
Your friend:	Is it 9th March?
You:	Yes, it is.

Let's see who finds your birthday first!

6 This is the sixth exercise (6th)

Everything about youth hostels

John and Toby know everything about youth hostels. John thinks that Toby is wrong and Toby, of course, thinks that John is wrong. John hates youth hostels. His friends Peter, Tim and Toby want to sleep in youth hostels next summer.

John und Toby haben völlig unterschiedliche Meinungen über Jugendherbergen. Toby ist von den Jugendherbergen begeistert. John hat anscheinend schlechte Erfahrungen gemacht und will sie nicht weiterempfehlen. Er möchte dich warnen und sagt dir, was dir während eines Jugendherbergsaufenthaltes alles passieren wird.

John says: The warden will rush into the bedroom at 7 o'clock in the morning.

Now you are John. Tell your friends about youth hostels.

The warden / not knock at your door
It / cost a lot of money
They / serve bad food
The tea / be too cold
The coffee / be too hot
Somebody / take your jeans
It / be difficult to find the youth hostels

But Toby says: You're wrong, Peter. Youth hostels are not as bad as that. The warden will welcome you at the door.

Now you are Toby:

The cook / hand you the menu
A waiter / serve you
The food / be really wonderful
The waiter / ask you: "Can I bring you another piece of cake, sir?"
Somebody / make the bed for you
The warden / say good night to you after supper
The warden / ask you: "Do you want to have breakfast in bed tomorrow morning?"
It / cost only £1 a day

Tim says: "Really, I can't believe it. I think it will be difficult to find a youth hostel like that."

7 This is the seventh exercise (7th)

After work

a) Here are some people and what they will do after work

Example:
You: What will Mr Green do after work?
Your friend: Mr Green will eat an apple.

eat an apple

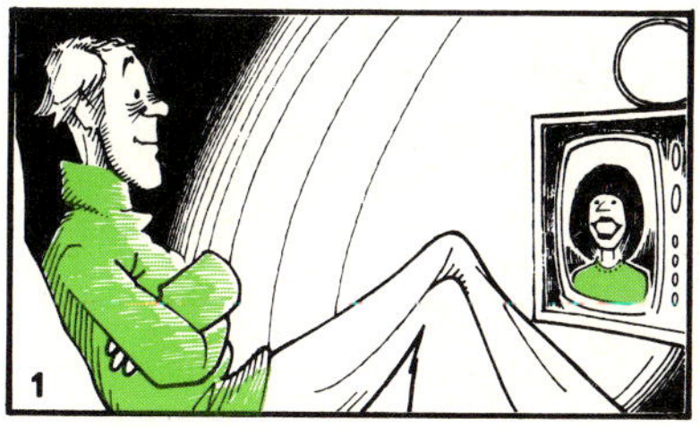

watch TV

read a book

work in the garden

eat a sausage

wash the car

drink tea

go to a restaurant

b) Now ask more questions.

Example:
Will Mr Green read a book after work?
No, he will eat an apple.

8 This is the eighth exercise (8th)

At the birthday party

At the birthday party the children play in the garden. Wendy asks questions. The boys and girls find the answers. It's a quiz. There are some nice **prizes** for good answers. Look at this poster.

Bei der Geburtstagsparty gibt es viele **Preise** zu gewinnen, wenn man bei einem Quiz die richtige Antwort gefunden hat. Schau dir das Bild an und sage, was dir besser gefällt.

a) The children look at the poster. A boy says: I think the football is nicer than the book. What do you think about these prizes?

b) At the end of the quiz the boys and the girls get the prizes:

Toby gets the record.
George gets the book.
Jean gets the poster of the pony.
Betty gets the football.
Susan gets the apple.
Linda gets the ball-point pen.
Tim gets the large piece of cake.

David and Hazel are unlucky. They don't get any prizes. David says "Toby is a lucky boy. He has got the 5th prize."
Go on: George ...

9 This is the ninth exercise (9th)

At the bus-stop

a) Look at these people. Who is taller, smaller, nicer, older, younger than the others?

Example: The third person is taller than the first person.

b) What are they wearing?

Example: The first lady is wearing a long dress and a hat.

Look at the other people and go on.

10 This is tenth exercise (10th)

Tomorrow Frau Schmidt will telephone her mother in Hamburg at 9 o'clock. How will she telephone?

First she ... (lift) the receiver. Then she ... (dial) 100 for Enquiries. The girl at Enquiries ... (give) her the code for Germany. It's 01049. Then the girl ... (tell) her how much ... (cost) for three minutes. Frau Schmidt ... (know) the code for Hamburg. It's 040. After that Frau Schmidt ... (dial) 01049—40 and her mother's number in Hamburg. Then she ... (say): Guten Abend, Mutti. Wie geht es dir?

11 This is the eleventh exercise (11th)

A game

There are twenty-six letters in the alphabet.

A	B	C	D	E	F	G	H	I	J	K	L	M	N	O	P	Q	R	S	T	U	V	W	X	Y	Z
1	2	3	4	5	6	7	8	9	10	11	12	13	14	15	16	17	18	19	20	21	22	23	24	25	26

a) *You:* Read the fifth letter of the alphabet.
Your friend: E is the fifth letter.

Now play this game in your class.

b) Another game with numbers:

You: Read the third line on the 26th page.

The first pupil who can answer goes on.

Now go on with:
You: Read the third word in the 3rd line on the 28th page.

Now go on with:
You: Read the third letter in the 5th word in the 12th line on the 68th page.

Vocabulary Definitions

a

Which day is today? Haven't you got a . . .?	Welchen Tag haben wir heute? Haben Sie keinen **Kalender**?	[ˈkælində]	*calendar*
Write the . . . for the garden party.	Schreibe die **Einladungskarten** für das Gartenfest / die Garten-Party.	[inviˈteiʃən kɑːd]	**invitation cards**
Telephone the food department and . . . the butter.	Ruf die Lebensmittelabteilung an und **bestelle** die Butter.	[ɔːdə]	**order** (to order)
I like bacon and . . . for breakfast. Salami is a . . .	Ich mag Speck und **Wurst** zum Frühstück. Salami ist eine **Wurst**.	[ˈsɔsidʒiz] [ˈsɔsidʒ]	**sausages** **sausage**
Please get the bread from the . . .	Bitte hol das Brot vom **Bäcker**.	[ˈbeikə]	**baker**

b

Ask the headmaster's . . .	Frag die **Sekretärin*** (den Sekretär) des Schulleiters.	[ˈsekritri]	*secretary*
Please show our guests . . . the school.	Bitte führen Sie unsere Gäste **durch** die Schule.	[raund]	**round**
We have fifteen guests. So we need 15 . . . dinners.	Wir haben fünfzehn Gäste. Also brauchen wir fünfzehn **zusätzliche** Mittagessen.	[ˈekstrə]	*extra*
I haven't got my calendar here. What's the . . . today?	Ich habe meinen Kalender nicht mit. Was ist das **Datum** von heute?	[deit]	**date**
I can show you the town . . . dinner.	Ich kann Sie **nach** dem Essen durch die Stadt führen.	[ˈɑːftə]	**after**

* Aus den englischen Berufsbezeichnungen kann man meist nicht erkennen, ob es ein Mann oder eine Frau ist.

c

Get the . . . Mr Smith is very ill.	Hol' die **Krankenschwester**. Herr Smith ist sehr krank.	[nə:s]	**nurse**
He is very ill. So he must go to . . .	Er ist sehr krank. Deshalb muß er ins **Krankenhaus**.	['hɔspitəl]	*hospital*
I must get up at 6 . . . the train leaves very early.	Ich muß um sechs aufstehen, **weil** der Zug sehr früh fährt.	[bi'kɔz]	**because**
Is there a parcel for me?	Ist da ein Paket für mich?		
No, not yet. The . . is late today.	Nein, noch nicht. Der **Briefträger** kommt heute sehr spät.	['pəustmən]	**postman**
There is Mr Brown's house.	Da ist Herrn Browns Haus.	[nɔk]	**knock**
Go on, . . . at the door.	Los, **klopf** an die Tür.		(to knock)
Have a . . . toast, dear.	Nimm doch **eine Scheibe** Toast.	['pi:s əv]	**piece of**
Can I have . . . piece of cake, please? I'm very hungry today.	Kann ich **noch ein** Stück Kuchen haben, bitte? Ich bin heute sehr hungrig.	[ə'nʌðə]	**another**
The next lesson . . . at ten o'clock.	Die nächste Stunde **fängt** um zehn an.	[sta:ts]	**starts** (to start)

d

Peter wants a German pen-friend. Perhaps his teacher knows . . .	Peter möchte einen deutschen Brieffreund haben. Vielleicht weiß sein Lehrer **jemanden**.	['sʌmbədi]	**somebody**
I don't know that girl. Please . . . me to her.	Ich kenne das Mädchen nicht. **Mach uns** doch bitte **miteinander bekannt**.	[intrə'dju:s]	**introduce** (to introduce)
Renate does not like English . . .	Renate mag das englische **Essen** nicht.	[fu:d]	**food**
English sausages are not the same; they are . . .	Englische Wurst ist nicht dasselbe. Sie ist **anders**.	['difrənt]	**different**
I can't telephone to Hamburg. I can't find the number and it's too . . .	Ich kann nicht nach Hamburg telefonieren. Ich kann die Nummer nicht finden und es ist zu **schwierig**.	['difikəlt]	**difficult**
First lift the . . .	Zuerst nehmen Sie den **Hörer** ab.	[ri'si:və]	**receiver**
I want to telephone New York.	Ich möchte New York anrufen.		
Please . . . the number for me.	Bitte **wählen** Sie die Nummer für mich.	['daiəl]	**dial** (to dial)
First . . . the receiver.	Zuerst **nehmen** Sie den Hörer **ab**.	[lift]	**lift** (to lift)
I'm afraid I don't know Mary's telephone number. Then you must dial . . .	Ich fürchte, ich weiß Marys Telefonnummer nicht. Dann mußt du die **Auskunft** wählen.	[in'kwaiəri:z]	**Enquiries**
I am in Oxford and I want to telephone somebody in London.	Ich bin in Oxford und ich möchte jemanden in London anrufen.		
Then you need the London . . . It is 01.	Dann brauchen Sie die **Vorwahl** von London. Sie ist 01.	[kəud]	code
This coat . . . £55.	Dieser Mantel **kostet** 55 Pfund.	[kɔst]	**costs** (to cost)
Hamburg is not . . . very far from London.	Hamburg ist **wirklich** nicht sehr weit von London.	['riəli]	**really**

Unit 5

a I don't mind

Mrs Moss: Don't forget, Carsten, you must tell us what you don't like. What about tea, for example? Perhaps you prefer coffee?
Carsten: You needn't worry, Mrs Moss. I really don't mind. I like tea, and I like coffee, too.
Mrs Moss: Fine. Do you take milk and sugar in your tea?
Carsten: No milk, thank you.
Wendy: Look what David is doing, Mum.
Mrs Moss: Don't be so silly, David. You mustn't take all the biscuits. Don't forget your father.

Questions

1 Which does Carsten prefer? Tea or coffee?
2 Does Carsten take milk in his tea?
3 Does Carsten take sugar in his tea?
4 What is David doing?
5 Why mustn't he do it?

Do you like English tea?

Example:
Mrs Hill: What about some tea? Or do you prefer coffee?
Carsten: I don't mind. I like tea and I like coffee.

Now it's your turn. Take the words from the list.

You: What about some ...? Or do you prefer ...?
Your partner: I don't mind. I like ..., and I like ..., too.

milk/lemonade, biscuits/cake, some ice-cream/pudding, toast/sandwiches

b Nunnery Wood School

1 The pupils of Nunnery Wood School in Worcester all have to wear a school uniform. The girls wear red skirts and awful school hats.

2 The boys are in red **blazers** and grey **trousers.**

3 The pupils have a **large playing-field.**

4 They have their dinner in the large **dining-hall.**

5 "Worcester Sauce" is the name of the school **magazine.**

6 It **describes important** things like **sports day.**

7 On the left you can see the school **clock,** and on the right an **alarm-clock.**

8 And that is the **bell** for the **end** of the **lesson**!

Questions

1 What do the girls have to wear?
2 What do the boys have to wear?
3 Where do the boys play football?
4 What do the pupils do in the large dining-hall?
5 What is "Worcester Sauce"?
6 What does it describe?
7 What can you see on the right?
8 What tells you that it's the end of the lesson?

Schools in England

The pupils of many schools have to wear (1)... The girls wear (2)... and (3)... and the boys wear (4)... and grey (5)... The pupils have their dinner at school. They go to the (6)...

C School uniform

1 *Speaker:* The last lesson of the day for form 2B is Maths. It starts at twenty past three and finishes at four o'clock.

2 *Maths teacher:* Where's your blazer, Tim? And why are you wearing a red shirt? You know you mustn't wear a red shirt to school.

3 *Tim Walker:* I'm against school uniform, sir. I think it's silly.

4 *Wendy:* The girls of the Cathedral school needn't wear silly school hats.

5 *Teacher:* Quiet a minute! What's that noise?

6 *Tim:* It's the bell, sir. Can we go home now?

7 *Teacher:* Don't be silly, Tim. It's an alarm-clock. Where is it? Ah, it's under that school magazine!

8 *Teacher:* What does this mean?
Wendy: Don't be angry, sir. Please open the magazine. On page 16 you'll find our letter about this awful uniform.

Questions

1 When does the Maths lesson finish?
2 What mustn't Tim do?
3 What does Tim think of the school uniform?
4 Why aren't the Cathedral School girls wearing school hats?
5 What does the teacher hear?
6 Where does Tim want to go?
7 Where is the alarm-clock?
8 What will the teacher find on page 16?

Schools in Germany

Tim Walker asks Carsten about German schools. Can you answer his questions?

1 Do you like school uniforms?
2 Do German pupils wear school uniforms?
2 Do you like our school uniform?
4 What do German pupils wear at school?
5 Don't you think school uniforms are silly? Why?
6 When does your school start on Mondays?
7 When do your lessons finish on Mondays?
8 Do you have school on Saturday?
9 When does your last lesson finish on Saturday?
10 Is it very quiet in your lessons or do pupils make a lot of noise?
11 Do you often write letters in the lessons?

d Can I have the Worcester Sauce, please

David: Can I have the Worcester Sauce, please, Wendy?
Wendy: Here you are, David.
David: Thank you.
Mrs Moss: Another piece of fish, Carsten?
Carsten: Yes, please.
Mrs Moss: Pass Carsten's plate, please, David, and give me the vegetables.

Questions

1 What does David ask for?
2 What does Mrs Moss offer Carsten?
3 Who wants Carsten's plate?
4 What does Mrs Moss ask for?

The children are hungry

Act this dialogue in your class.

Wendy: Can I have the ... please? (sugar / butter / chips / sandwiches)
David: Here you are, Eileen.
Mrs Harris: ..., Carsten? (Another piece of cake / Some more toast / Another piece of fish / Another cup of tea)
Carsten: Yes, please.
Mrs Harris: Pass Carsten's plate please, and hand me the ... (milk / tea / lemonade / tray)

Grammar Practice

1 A can't – mustn't – needn't

"Please, Mum, **can** I get a new football?"
"No, you **can't.**"

"You **needn't** do any homework today."

"You mustn't do that."
"Go away. **Don't** play here.

1 B

Can I go now?	Yes, you **can.** (= kannst) No, you **can't.** (= darfst nicht oder kannst nicht) No, you **mustn't.** (= darfst nicht)
Must I help?	Yes, you **must.** No, you **needn't.** (= brauchst nicht)

can + not = cannot = can't
must + not = mustn't
need + not = needn't
do + not = don't

1 C

Answers the questions:

An English boy is asking a German girl.

1 Must you wear school uniforms in Germany? No, we ...
2 Must you do homework for school? Yes, we ...
3 Must you learn English at school? Yes, we ...
4 Must you go to school in the afternoon? No, we ...
5 Must ...? ...

Exercises

1 Mrs Hill's first driving-lesson

a) What does Mr Hill say?

Example:
Mr Hill: Don't turn right.

turn right

Now you are Mr Hill. Tell Mrs Hill what she mustn't do.

stop

drive too fast

overtake

turn left

sleep

park here

follow that bike

drive into that filling-station

do that again

b) Mr und Mrs Brown fahren hinter dem Wagen der Hills her. Mr Brown wundert sich über die Fahrweise von Mrs Hill. Er redet mit seiner Frau darüber.

Example:	What's the matter with that car?
	It mustn't stop here.
or:	What is she doing?
	She mustn't turn right.

What else does Mr Brown say? Go on!

2 Don't!

Fathers, mothers, brothers, sisters, teachers, policemen very often say:
Don't do that! You can't do that! You mustn't do that!

1 You mustn't sit on the table!
2 You mustn't eat too many cakes!
3 You can't eat all that!
4 You can't wear that awful hat!
5 You mustn't talk like that!
6 You can't eat dog food!
7 You mustn't play football in the front-garden!
8 You can't drink petrol!
9 You mustn't be late!
10 You can't watch TV today!

Now say the sentences like this:

1 Don't sit on the table, please!
2 Don't ...

3 Must I really wear it?

Mother and Betty are standing in Betty's room and talking about Betty's clothes.

Example:

...this pullover?...

Betty: Must I really wear this pullover? It's so hot today.
Mother: No, you needn't wear it.

Find the correct questions and answers.

1 ...this school uniform? ... 

2 ...this old coat? ... 

3 ...that blue blazer? ... 

4 ...this summer dress? ... 

5 ...that long skirt? ... 

6 ...this white pullover? ... 

7 ...these black shoes? ... 

8 ...these new white jeans? ... 

4 A Sunday with the Blacks

The Blacks have 6 children. They ask a lot of questions.

Fill in must, mustn't, needn't, don't.

Bob: ... I wear this school uniform today?
Mother: No, you ...
Susan: ... I wash my hands now?
Father: Yes, you ...
Father: Oh dear! Timmy! What are you doing? ... play with the Worcester Sauce.
George: ... I clean your car today?
Father: No, you ...
Mother: Tina, ... clean your bike in the living-room. You ... go outside.
Tina: ... I really go out? It's raining outside.
Mother: No, you ..., but you ... clean your bike in the house.
Toby: Mother is cooking in the kitchen. ... she always do everything?
Father: No, she ... Why ... you help her?
Hazel: Daddy, you ... read the book now. Toby, you ... play with the dog. Why ... we all help her? It's Sunday today.

5 Peter can't help his mother

Talk to your partner.

Example:

Talk to your partner.

Can you help ...

your sister?
Father in the garden?
me in the kitchen?
that foreigner, he can't find his hotel?
that postman, he can't open that door?

No, I can't. I must ...

go to the baker's first
help Father
read this magazine first
finish my Maths homework
finish this page in my book
do my homework
introduce my friend Jim to Father
telephone Enquiries to get the code for Germany

But you needn't do that now.
You can do that ...

tomorrow
next week
on Sunday
after dinner
in the morning
in the evening

6 HDYD CS 2 Textbook 42920

6 Comprehension Exercise

A letter to Germany

Dear Mother and Father,

I'm writing in English. I want to show you that my English is getting better every day. I'm very happy with the Moss family. They're all very nice. Mrs Moss likes me and I like her, too. Mr Moss always forgets my name, but that doesn't matter.

Their children, David and Wendy are my friends now. I like them very much. They always help me when I forget a difficult word. English food is different from our food. I prefer the food at home.

At school the children must be very quiet. There is no noise in the classroom. The teachers need not shout. At 12 o'clock the bell rings, the lesson ends and all the children go to the dining-hall.

The school meals are not very good, but we can have a lot of vegetables. The school-meal costs only 25p every day.

For English boys and girls the school uniform is something very important. In Nunnery Wood School the boys must wear grey trousers, black shoes, red blazers, a white shirt and a tie. The girls must wear red skirts and awful school hats.

David hates his school uniform because he must wear it at school every day. I'm glad that we need not wear school uniforms in Germany.

Somebody is knocking at the door. I must stop here.

Love,
Carsten

Find the correct answer:

1 Who is writing this letter?
a) Tom
b) Uwe
c) Carsten
d) David

2 He is writing from
a) London
b) Worcester
c) Hamburg
d) Germany

3 He is writing to
a) England
b) Hamburg
c) Worcester
d) London

4 He is living with the
a) Moss family
b) Schmidt family
c) Cartwright family
d) Brown family

5 Who forgets Carsten's name?
a) David's father
b) David's sister
c) Wendy's brother
d) David's mother

6 At 12 o'clock the boys and girls eat
a) at home
b) in the classroom
c) in the dining-hall
d) in a restaurant

7 Boys in Nunnery Wood School must wear
a) green blazers, white shoes, and a tie
b) red blazers, a tie and a school hat
c) grey blazers, red trousers and black shoes
d) white shirts, red blazers and grey trousers

Questions

1 Does Carsten like the Moss family?
2 What does Mr Moss always forget?
3 Does Carsten like English food?
4 Where do the pupils have school dinner?
5 How much is the school-meal for the boys and girls?
6 Can boys go to school with brown shoes?
7 Can girls go to school in blue jeans?
8 Why is Carsten writing this letter in English?

Vocabulary Definitions

a

You must do your homework today. Please don't . . .!	Du mußt heute deine Hausaufgaben machen. **Vergiß** es bitte nicht!	[fəˈgət]	**forget** (to forget)
I hate English food: English sausages . . .	Ich mag das englische Essen überhaupt nicht: **zum Beispiel** englische Wurst.	[fərigˈzaːmpl]	**for example**
I don't like tea. I . . . coffee.	Ich mag keinen Tee. Ich **mag lieber** Kaffee.	[priˈfəː]	**prefer** (to prefer)
I'm very sorry. Don't . . .. It's OK.	Das tut mir aber leid. **Keine Ursache**. Das ist schon in Ordnung.	[ˈwʌri]	**worry** (to worry)
I can't come on Monday. That's OK. I really . . .	Ich kann Montag nicht kommen. Das ist in Ordnung. Es **macht** mir wirklich nichts **aus**.	[dəunt maind]	**don't mind** (to mind)

b

A lot of English boys wear . . . for school.	Viele englische Jungen ziehen für die Schule einen **Blazer** an.	[ˈbleizəz]	*blazers*
English boys wear blazers and grey . . .	Englische Jungen ziehen in der Schule Blazer und graue **Hosen** an.	[ˈtrauzəz]	**trousers**
The opposite for 'small' is . . .	Das Gegenteil von 'klein' ist **'groß'**.	[laːdʒ]	**large**
The pupils play football on their . . .	Die Schüler spielen auf ihrem **Sportplatz** Fußball	[ˈpleiŋ fiːld]	**playing-field**
They have their dinner in the . .	Sie essen Mittag im **Speisesaal**.	[ˈdainiŋ hɔːl]	*dining-hall*
Carsten wants to write a story for the school . . .	Carsten möchte eine Geschichte für die **Schulzeitung** schreiben.	[mægəˈziːn]	*magazine*
He wants to . . . a day at his Hamburg school.	Er möchte einen Tag in seiner Hamburger Schule **beschreiben**.	[disˈkraib]	**describe** (to describe)
The magazine describes . . . things like . . .	Die Schulzeitung schreibt über **wichtige** Dinge wie **Sportfeste**.	[imˈpɔːtənt] [ˈspɔːtsdei]	**important** *sports day*
The pupils know what time it is; they have a big school . . .	Die Schüler wissen, wie spät es ist; sie haben eine große Schul**uhr**.	[klɔk]	**clock**
You are late every morning! You must buy an . . .	Du kommst jeden Morgen zu spät. Du mußt dir einen **Wecker** kaufen.	[əˈlaːmklɔk]	*alarm-clock*
Listen! That's the school . . .	Horch mal. Das ist die Schul**glocke**.	[bel]	**bell**
We must hurry up!	Wir müssen uns beeilen.		
All right, you can go now.	Das wär's, ihr könnt jetzt gehen.	[end]	**end**
That's the . . . of the . . .	Das ist der **Schluß** der **Stunde**.	[lesn]	**lesson**

c

The opposite of 'first' is . . .	Das Gegenteil von der (die, das) Erste ist der (die, das) **Letzte**.	[lɑːst]	**last**
Tim is in . . . 2B for his lessons.	Tim ist in seinen Schulstunden in **Klasse** 2B.	[fɔːm]	**form**
What is 1789x96, Tim? Ah, he is in the . . . lesson now.	Wieviel ist 1 789 x 96? Ach ja, er ist jetzt in der **Mathe**(matik)-Stunde.	[mæθs]	*Maths*
The lesson starts at 11 and . . . at 11.45.	Die Stunde fängt um 11 an und **hört** um 11.45 **auf**.	[finiʃiz]	**finishes** (to finish)
Tim does not like his school uniform. He is . . . school uniforms.	Tim mag seine Schuluniform nicht. Er ist **gegen** eine Schuluniform.	[ə'genst]	**against**
'You are making too much . . .!	Ihr macht zuviel **Krach/Lärm**.	[nɔiz]	**noise**
Be . . ., please!'	Seid **ruhig**, bitte.	[kwaiət]	**quiet**
Why are you late again, John Smith? Please don't . . ., sir.	Warum kommst du schon wieder zu spät, John Smith? **Seien Sie** bitte nicht **böse**, Sir.	[bi'æŋgri]	**be angry** (to be angry)
Open your books. We are on . . 18.	Schlagt die Bücher auf. Wir sind auf **Seite 18.**	[peidʒ]	**page**
want to write a . . . to my penriend.	Ich möchte einen **Brief** an meine Brieffreundin schreiben.	['letə]	**letter**

d

Can I have the Worcester . . ., please?	Kann ich bitte die Worcester-**Soße** haben?	[sɔːs]	*sauce*
Another cake, Tim? Then . . . me your plate, please.	Dann **reich** mir bitte deinen Teller.	[pɑːs]	**pass** (to pass)
Tomatoes and peas are . . .	Tomaten und Erbsen sind **Gemüse**.	['vedʒitəblz]	**vegetables**

It's sports day. These girls are playing basketball.

Revision Unit I

Where is that girl Hannelore?

Frau Schmidt: Do you know where Hannelore is? We can't find her.
Herr Henning: But that's awful. Where can she be? Doesn't her Worcester friend know where she is?
Frau Schmidt: No, she doesn't. I'll telephone the police, I think.
Herr Henning: No, you mustn't do that yet. Let's ask all the boys and girls in our group. Perhaps they can find her. Then we needn't tell the police and I needn't telephone her family.

At four o'clock on that Friday, 23rd July, all the children are sitting in a classroom in the Worcester school. Herr Henning is speaking to the headmaster. Frau Schmidt is explaining everything to Mrs Bennett, the school secretary.

Herr Henning: "Quiet, please. You all know Hannelore. She's quite tall and has fair hair. She's wearing a black skirt and a green blazer. Do you know where she can be?"

Else: "Excuse me, Herr Henning, Hannelore loves English cakes. I say she is in the cafeteria in Malvern Road."

Gerda: I don't agree. Hannelore must be at a Pop Concert. She likes good music better than cakes. I think she wants to hear 'The Marmalade' pop group in Birmingham.

Herr Henning: I don't believe that.

Secretary: Ah, there's the telephone. Excuse me, please.

Three minutes later

Herr Henning: Don't worry, Frau Schmidt.

Frau Schmidt: I'm not worried. I'm angry. Hannelore is a silly girl. She knows she mustn't leave Worcester.

Secretary: You needn't worry. Hannelore is all right. I've got old Mrs Manson on the telephone. She's got Hannelore at her house here in Worcester. Hannelore is working in her garden. You know, Mrs Manson is too old for that. And now she wants to know — can Hannelore stay with her for tea?

Herr Henning: She's a nice girl, that Hannelore. I always say, we worry too much. Isn't that right, Frau Schmidt?

Frau Schmidt: Oh well, why can't she tell us when she wants to do something alone. Listen, children .....

Questions

1 Who is Frau Schmidt looking for?
2 What does Frau Schmidt think she'll do?
3 What does Herr Henning want to do first?
4 Who is in the classroom on that Friday?
5 What is the date on that Friday?
6 What is Frau Schmidt doing at that time?
7 What does Hannelore look like?
8 What is Hannelore wearing?
9 Why does Gerda think she must be at a Pop Concert?
10 Why is Mrs Manson telephoning the school secretary?
11 What does Herr Henning always say?
12 Does Frau Schmidt agree with him?

Birmingham ['bə:miŋəm]

Exercises

1 Grandmother doesn't understand

Eileen erzält ihrer Großmutter von der Schule. Oma hört jedoch sehr schlecht. Manche Einzelheiten (die im Text **fett** gedruckt sind) versteht sie nicht, deshalb muß sie laufend nachfragen.

Example:

Eileen: **In June** we play games.
Grandmother: When do you play games?
Eileen: In June.

Now you ask grandmother's questions.

1 *Eileen:* We always wear **this awful school uniform.**
2 *Eileen:* I hate those **blue skirts.**
3 *Eileen:* **At three o'clock** we always play tennis.
4 *Eileen:* In the morning we often **play hockey.**
5 *Eileen:* We always play football on the **playing-field.**
6 *Eileen:* At 12 o'clock we have our dinner in the **large dining-room.**

2 How many questions can you ask?

Example: On Sundays (1) I (2) have breakfast (3) in bed (4) at 9 o'clock (5).

1 *You:* When do you have breakfast in bed?
Your friend: On Sundays.
2 *You:* Who has breakfast in bed?
Your friend: I do. / I have breakfast in bed.
3 *You:* What do you have in bed?
Your friend: Breakfast.
4 *You:* Where do you have breakfast on Sundays?
Your friend: In bed.
5 *You:* When do you have breakfast on Sundays?
Your friend: At 9 o'clock.

Now it's your turn.

On Saturdays (1) I (2) get up (3) at 7 o'clock (4).

On Fridays (1) Susan (2) gets home (3) from school at 4 o'clock (4).

On Thursdays (1) Brian (2) always watches (3) TV (4) in the evening (5).

3 Mr Robert's calendar

Mr Roberts is very busy. Here is what he does every year.

JAN	London	JULY	Germany
FEB	Worcester	AUG	New York
MAR	Hamburg	SEPT	Stuttgart
APR	France	OCT	U.S.A
MAY	Dover	NOV	Oxford
JUNE	Harwich	DEC	Glasgow

Now ask your neighbour.

Examples:

1 Where does Mr Roberts go in March?
2 When does he go to London?
3 What does he do in April?

4 Miller's cars are better!

a) Mr Brown wants to buy a car. He and Mrs Brown are looking at these cars at Miller's Garage. Here is what they say.

Example:

Mrs Brown:	These cars are very nice. How much is the first car?
Mr Miller:	It's £2,300.
Mrs Brown:	How much is the second car?
Mr Miller:	...

Go on and talk to your partner:

b) Now Mr Brown and Mrs Brown are talking about all the cars.

Example:

Mr Brown: The fifth car is very nice.
Mrs Brown: But the fourth car is cheaper than the fifth car.
Mr Brown: You are right. And the third car is cheaper than the fourth car.
Mrs Brown: I see. But the ...
Mr Brown: You are quite right. ...
Mr Miller: Don't forget. A bike is much cheaper than my cars.

Now go on and talk about these cars.

c) Now draw the cars on the board and act this scene.
Look at the pictures and compare the cars. Use: older, faster, cheaper, nicer ...

d) *Mr Brown:* Bikes aren't very fast. Cars are faster than bikes.
Mrs Brown: Yes, and the first car is faster than a bike.
Mr Brown: But look here. The second car is ... than ...
Mr Miller: Don't forget. The second car is ...
Mrs Brown: You are right. And the third car is ...
Mr Miller: And I like the fourth car. It's ...
Mr Brown: But I like the fifth car. It's ... than police cars.

e) Now you are Mr and Mrs Brown. Compare the cars and use forms of the words: old, nice, big, cheap, safe, new

Begin like this:

Mr Brown: I want to buy the ... car. It's ... than the ... car. And it's ... than...
Mrs Brown: But the ... car is ... than the ... car ...

5 Can you find the words?

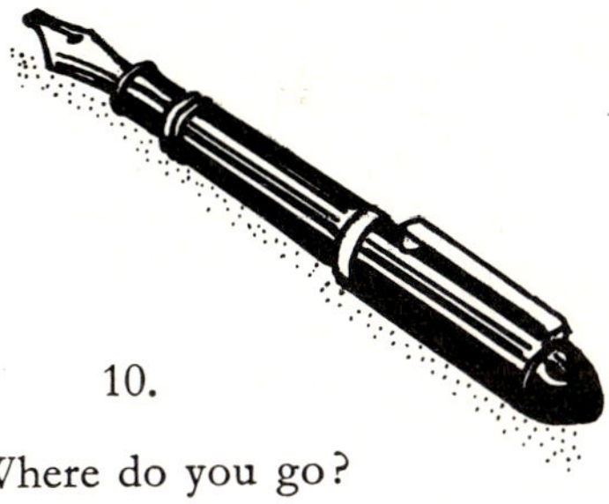

a) At the station

1 You have lost your wallet. Where do you go?
2 That man wants to see your tickets. Who is he?
3 You put your trousers and shirts into it.
4 The train to Dover leaves from  10.
5 You are on the train to Dover. You are hungry. Where do you go?
6 This is a new  The seats are very nice.
7 A man says over the  "The train will be 20 minutes late."

b) At the department store

What can you buy there?
The boy or the girl who can write down the most things in two minutes is the winner.

c) **British schools**

Can you complete this?

The boys and girls must wear ..[redacted]. The boys wear .[redacted] and [redacted].
The girls wear skirts and awful [redacted] At 12 o'clock they have lunch in the ...

Today is their sports day.

They play games in the ... The girls play ... and the boys play. ... ... 3b is the winner in the ... match. Then the ... rings. "See you tomorrow," they say. They will come back to school at a quarter to 9. The pupils can read the story about the sports day in the school ...

6 Before — After

a) Look at these pictures. In picture 1 Mr M. is not strong. His legs are not strong, his arms are not strong. His hands and feet are small and his neck is not strong.

Now look at picture 2.
Mr M.'s legs are very strong.
His arms are ...
His ...

b) Now compare your neighbour with Mr M. in the second picture.

> *Example:* Mr M.'s arms are bigger than Peter's.

c) Now tell your friend to go there. He will get as strong as Mr M.

> *Example:* After five weeks your hands will be stronger than today. You will be as strong as Mr M.

7 English and German pupils

Make up sentences.

English children English boys English girls German boys German girls German children	don't mustn't needn't must	wear school uniforms be quiet in the lessons wear black trousers eat in the dining-hall wear school hats wear blue blazers have dinner at home wear blue shirts play football in their school uniforms wear blue jeans at school

8 An American in England

Many people think Americans always say:

Everything is better in the U.S.A.

a) Now you are an American tourist.

Our American	boats suitcases coaches dining-cars ticket collectors sausages secretaries trousers food hospitals houses department stores motorways cars	is are	faster heavier hungrier nicer newer tidier taller better	than your English...

b) Sometimes you think the American is right.

You say: "Yes, you're right. English boats aren't as fast as American boats."

Now go on.

c) Sometimes you think he is wrong.

You say: No, that's wrong. English cars are as fast as American cars.

Unit 6

a In Cornwall

1 Tim Carter is thirteen, and a Worcester boy.

2 His mother Jean and her husband Norman are with him on holiday.

3 They are at a small hotel in **Falmouth,** Cornwall.

4 Tim is tall for his **age** and has black hair and blue **eyes.**

5 He likes Maths and he reads a lot about sport and trains.

6 He is a very good **swimmer** and he wants to be a cook in a hotel.

Questions

1 How old is Tim Carter?
Where does Tim live?
2 Who is Norman?
3 Where are they staying?
4 What does Tim look like?
5 What does Tim like to read?
6 What does Tim want to be?

b A trip to Land's End

Manager: Are you coming back for lunch today, Mr Carter?
Mr Carter: No, we're off to Land's End.
The Browns are taking us on a trip in their car.
Manager: Well, I hope it will stay fine for you.
Mr Carter: You never know in the West of England. It always rains.
We're going to take our raincoats.
Manager: Do you need any sandwiches?
Mr Carter: No, thank you. We're going to have a meal in a restaurant.

Questions

1 Why is Mr Carter not coming back for lunch today?
2 Who is taking him there?
3 What does the manager hope?
4 Why is Mr Carter taking his raincoat?
5 Why doesn't Mr Carter need any sandwiches?

Don't forget the sausages

Peter's school will visit Land's End tomorrow. His mother wants to know what he needs for the trip.

Talk to your partner:

...an orange.
...biscuits for lunch.
...sandwiches for dinner.
...

His mother thinks he will need more things.

Mother: Don't forget to take five sausages.
Peter: I'm not going to take any sausages.

Now go on with: your new suitcase, your two pullovers, your alarm-clock, your bike.

Now act this scene.

C What are your plans for tomorrow?

Mr Brown: What are your plans for tomorrow? Are you going to watch the football?
Mr Carter: No, we're going to pack. We're driving back to Worcester the day after tomorrow.
Have you got any plans?
Mr Brown: Yes, we're going to visit Longleat. Then we're going to have a meal in a restaurant.
Mr Carter: Oh, that's nice.
Mr Brown: You can't just stay here on your last day. Why not come with us? You can pack in the evening.
Mr Carter: Yes, why not. That's a good idea! Thank you very much!

Questions

1 Why is Mr Carter not going to watch the football?
2 Where is he driving to the day after tomorrow?
3 What are Mr Brown's plans for the next day?
4 When can Mr Carter pack?
5 What does Mr Carter think of Mr Brown's idea?

What are your plans for tomorrow?

Talk to your partner.

watch television?
visit London?
see Longleat House?
have lunch at the hotel?

pack our suitcases.
see Land's End.
have lunch at a cafeteria.
visit Mr Brown in Oxford.

Are you going to see the lions at Longleat?

d The Lions of Longleat

Longleat is a **beautiful old** house in the West of England.
On one **side** of the house there is a cafeteria.
It **sells** oranges, sandwiches and **rolls**.
On the **other** side there are three **call-boxes**.
In the large **park** there are a lot of **lions**.
The tourists drive **through** the park and look at the lions.
The cars have to leave the park **by** seven o'clock.

Questions

1 What is Longleat?
2 Where is the cafeteria?
3 Where are the call-boxes?
4 Where are the lions?
5 What do the tourists do?
6 When do the cars have to leave?

At Windsor Safari Park

This is a ... house. On one ... of the house there is a ... They sell ... ... and ... On the ... side there are two ... Three tourists are going to see the ... in the park.
Many tourists drive ... the park every day. The cars have to leave ... seven o'clock.

side oranges and sandwiches beautiful call-boxes by rolls through lions cafeteria

The picnic

The next day, the Carters and the Browns drive to Longleat. They leave the car in the park and sit under a big tree. There they have a lovely picnic — ham rolls, a big meat-pie, sandwiches and a lot of cold lemonade and oranges.
After the picnic they go back to the car park and get into the car. They are going to see the lions now, and Mr Brown wants to take a lot of photographs with his new camera.

7 HDYD CS 2 Textbook 42920

They drive through the park. The other people are having lunch in the cafeteria. So the park is empty. There are only the Browns and the Carters in the park — and, of course, the lions.
Then the car stops. "What's the matter? Do you want to take another photograph?" Mrs Brown asks.
"No, I don't," Mr Brown answers. "I can't understand it. Why doesn't the car start again, darling?"
"I know why not," Tim tells him. "Look, your petrol tank is empty."
"Oh, dear, what are we going to do?" the two women shout. "Look, those three lions are coming towards our car. Close the windows!"
The three large lions come and look at the five people in the car.
"They're going to eat us," shouts Mrs Brown.
The lions look at Mrs Brown and walk away. "Silly woman," they think.
And then the park warden arrives in a lorry. He's got a tin of petrol on his lorry. So everything is all right, and they are back at the hotel by seven o'clock.

Questions

1 Where do the Carters drive to?
2 Where do they leave the car?
3 What do they do under the big tree?
4 What do they do after the picnic?
5 What does Mr Brown want to do with his new camera?
6 What are the other people doing in the cafeteria?
7 Who is in the park now?
8 Why does Mr Brown's car stop?
9 Why are the two women shouting?
10 How many lions are there?
11 What do the lions do?
12 Who arrives in a lorry?
13 Why can he help?
14 When do the Carters arrive back at the hotel?

Grammar Practice

1 A going to . . . / I'm coming . . .

"My friend **is coming** next week."

"Look, Mr Benson **is going to buy** a dog."

"I think **I'll** eat a ham roll this afternoon."

1 B

He's	coming	next week.
They are	driving	back tomorrow.

We're		visit London.
I'm	going to	to have breakfast in a hotel.
He's		to buy a dog.

In Unit 4 hatten wir die erste Futur-Form kennengelernt:
I think **I'll** eat a ham roll this afternoon. = 'll-Futur
Diese Futur-Form verwendet man, wenn man sich in diesem Augenblick oder kurz vorher entscheidet.
Nun gibt es noch zwei weitere Formen, mit denen wir die Zukunft ausdrücken können:
He's com**ing** next week. = ing-Form
Diese Futur-Form verwendet man, wenn eine ganz feste Abmachung besteht.
He's **going to buy** a dog. = going to + verb
Die dritte Futur-Form verwendet man, wenn eine feste Absicht schon länger vorliegt.

1 C ing-form / going to + verb

1 Here's a letter from Carsten. He (come) . . . next week.
2 There's a football match tomorrow. Peter (watch) . . . it on TV.
3 We must go to Sally's party. She (invite) ... all her friends tomorrow.
4 Susan has got £2 now. She (buy) . . . a record.
5 Mr Carter has got plans for tomorrow. He (have) . . . a lovely picnic.

Exercises

1 What are you going to do tomorrow?

Ask your friends about their plans for tomorrow.
These pictures will help you.

Example:

You:	What are you going to do tomorrow afternoon?
Your friend:	I'm going to play football.

2 Going to Land's End

Father writes down what the children have to do before they can start. Here is Father's list:

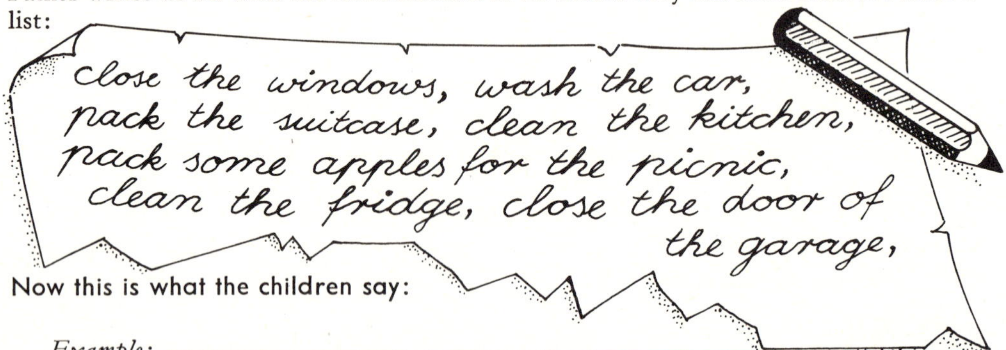

Now this is what the children say:

Example:

Johnny: I'm going to wash the car this afternoon but I'm not going to clean the kitchen.

What do Betty, Susan, Jerry, Tom say?

3 Where are you going to buy your jeans?

Look at the pictures on p. 47 and ask questions.

Example: jeans / them / cheap

This list will help you. Now go on:

skirt / it / long
pullover / it / warm
nightdress / it / nice
swimsuit / it / pretty
summer dress / it / short
suit / it / cheap

4 Plans for a trip

Tim is telling his mother what he and his friends are going to do at Longleat tomorrow. He wants to get some pocket money for the trip. So he tells her everything about the trip. What does he say to his mother? The longer you speak the more money you'll get.

Tim möchte bei seiner Mutter Taschengeld für den Ausflug „lockermachen". Um sie von der Notwendigkeit zu überzeugen, muß er ziemlich lange reden und viele Gründe anführen. Je länger er redet und je überzeugender er spricht, desto mehr Taschengeld bekommt er.

First we are going to ...	walk through the park
then we are ...	watch the lions
after that ...	visit the beautiful house
after lunch ...	go to the cafeteria on one side of the house
after that ...	go to the shop on the other side of the house
in the afternoon ...	have a picnic with sandwiches, rolls and oranges
and then ...	leave Longleat by 4 o'clock
in the evening ...	be back by 6 o'clock

Now do it again. Close your books.

5 Our holiday

Talk to your partner.

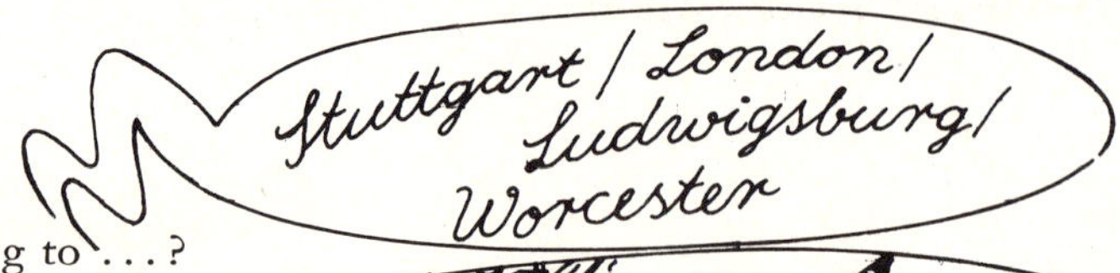

Partner: How are you going to . . . ?

You: Oh, I'm going by . . .

Partner: When are you leaving ?

You: At . . . from . . .

6 What are you going to be? ■

Your teacher wants to know what you are going to be after you leave school. Look at these pictures and answer your teacher's question: "What are you going to be when you leave school?"

Example:

Teacher: What are you going to be when you leave school?
You: I'm going to be a policeman.

Now look at the pictures and go on.

Vocabulary Definitions

a

Tim Carter		['tim 'kɑ:tə]	**Tim Carter**
Jean		[dʒi:n]	**Jean**
Norman		['nɔ:mən]	**Norman**
Falmouth		['fælməθ]	**Falmouth**
Cornwall		['kɔ:nwɔl]	**Cornwall**
What is your . . .? I'm fifteen.	Wie **alt** bist du? Ich bin fünfzehn.	[eidʒ]	**age**
You see with your . . .	Du siehst mit deinen **Augen**.	[aiz]	**eyes**
She wants to buy a new swimsuit. She is a very good . . ., you know.	Sie möchte sich einen neuen Badeanzug kaufen. Weißt du, sie ist eine sehr gute **Schwimmerin**.	['swimə]	*swimmer*

b

We're going to Cornwall. We're making a . . . to . . .	Wir fahren nach Cornwall. Wir machen dort einen **Ausflug** nach **Land's End** (das ist die Südwestspitze von England).	[trip] ['lændz'end]	*trip* **Land's End**
Breakfast is at 8 and . . . is at 1 o'clock.	Frühstück gibt es um acht und **Mittagessen** um eins.	[lʌntʃ]	**lunch**
Tim is leaving the house now. He . . . . school.	Tim verläßt jetzt das Haus. Er **geht los** zur Schule.	[iz ɔf tu:]	**is off to** (to be off to)
The weather is fine.	Es ist schönes Wetter.		
I . . . it stays fine for you.	Ich **hoffe**, es bleibt schön für euch.	[həup]	**hope** (to hope)
Cornwall and Land's End are in the . . . of England.	Cornwall und Land's End liegen im **Westen** Englands.	[west]	*West*
It's not going to stay fine. You must take your . . .	Es bleibt nicht schön. Ihr müßt eure **Regenmäntel** mitnehmen.	['reinkəuts]	**raincoats**
I need some bread, some butter and some tomatoes for the . . .	Ich brauche einiges an Brot, an Butter und an Tomaten für die **belegten Brote**.	['sændwitʃiz]	*sandwiches*

c

What are you going to do in the holidays? What are your . . . for the holidays?	Was habt ihr vor in den Ferien? Was sind eure **Pläne** für die Ferien?	[plænz]	*plans*
Today is Tuesday, tomorrow is Wednesday and . . . is Thursday.	Heute ist Dienstag, morgen ist Mittwoch, und **übermorgen** ist Donnerstag.	[dei ɑ:ftə tə'mɔrəu]	**the day after tomorrow**
Longleat		['lɔŋli:t]	**Longleat**
I like that. That's a good . . .!	Das finde ich gut. Das ist ein guter **Vorschlag**.	[ai'di:ə]	**idea**

d

There are a lot of . . . at Longleat.	Es gibt viele **Löwen** in Longleat.	[laiənz]	**lions**
She is a very pretty girl. Yes, she is . . .	Sie ist ein sehr hübsches Mädchen. Ja, sie ist **schön.**	['bju:tiful]	**beautiful**
There is a cafeteria on one . . . of the house.	Es gibt ein Selbstbedienungsrestaurant auf der einen **Seite** des Hauses.	[said]	**side**

Excuse me, do you . . . oranges in this shop?	Verzeihung, **verkaufen** Sie Apfelsinen in diesem Geschäft?	[sel]	**sell** (to sell)
The English have toast for breakfast. A lot of Germans have . . . for breakfast.	Die Engländer essen zum Frühstück Toast. Viele Deutsche essen **Brötchen** zum Frühstück.	[rəulz] [rəul]	**rolls** **roll**
On this side there is a cafeteria, and on the . . . side there is the park.	Auf dieser Seite ist ein Selbstbedienungsrestaurant, und auf der **anderen** Seite ist der Park.	[ˈʌðə]	**other**
Where can I telephone, please? Oh, there is a . . . over there.	Wo kann ich bitte telefonieren? Da drüben ist eine **Telefonzelle**.	[ˈkɔːlbɔks]	**call-box**
Where are you going with your baby? Oh, I'm taking him to Hyde . . .	Wohin gehen Sie mit ihrem Baby? Ach, ich gehe mit ihm zum Hyde **Park**.	[pɑːk]	*park*
Where is Windsor Street, please? It's at the other end of town. So you must go . . . the town.	Wo ist die Windsor-Straße bitte? Sie ist auf dem anderen Ende der Stadt. Also müssen Sie durch die Stadt **hindurch** gehen/fahren.	[θruː]	**through**
Don't leave yet. It's early! Sorry, I must be home . . . seven, and not later.	Geh noch nicht weg. Es ist noch früh. Tut mir leid, ich muß **gegen** sieben zu Hause sein, nicht später.	[bai]	**by**

e

The day after that: the . . . day.	Der Tag danach: der **nächste** Tag.	[nekst]	**next**
We're having our lunch in the park: We're having a lot of sandwiches and lemonade: we're having a . . .	Wir essen im Park zu Mittag: Wir essen eine Menge belegter Brote und trinken Brause: wir machen ein **Picknick**.	[ˈpiknik]	*picnic*
Do you want a cheese roll? No, I prefer a . . . roll.	Möchtest du ein Käsebrötchen? Nein, ich nehme lieber ein **Schinken**brötchen.	[hæm]	**ham**
The Carters are having a big meat . . . for their picnic.	Die Carters essen eine große Fleisch**pastete** zum Picknick.	[pai]	**pie**
I want a photograph of that lion there. Where is your . . .?	Ich möchte ein Foto von dem Löwen dort. Wo ist dein **Fotoapparat**?	[ˈkæmərə]	*camera*
What about my question? Why don't you . . . it?	Wie ist es mit meiner Frage? Warum **beantwortest** du sie nicht?	[ˈɑːnsə]	**answer** (to answer)
It's cold. Look that window is open. Please . . . it.	Es ist kalt. Guck mal, das Fenster ist offen. **Mach** es bitte **zu**.	[kləuz]	**close** (to close)
The lions walk to the other side. They walk . . .	Die Löwen gehen zur anderen Seite. Sie gehen **weg**.	[əˈwei]	**away**
I can't take this furniture in my van. You need a big . . .	Ich kann diese Möbel in meinem Lieferwagen nicht mitnehmen. Sie brauchen einen großen **Lastwagen**.	[ˈlɔri]	**lorry**
Travemünde is at the . . .	Travemünde liegt an der **See**.	[ˈsiːˈsaid]	**seaside**

a Mrs Brown is very angry!

1 *Mrs Brown:* Where are you, Cecil?
Mr Brown: I'm in the kitchen, dear.

2 *Mrs Brown:* And where have you been?
Mr Brown: **I've been** in the garden.

3 *Mrs Brown:* Are you washing those plates now?
Mr Brown: **I've** just **washed** them.

4 *Mrs Brown:* And when are you starting the supper?
Mr Brown: **I've** already **started** it, dear.

5 *Mrs Brown:* Good. Now, what about the party on Thursday? Have you telephoned the Blakes yet?
Mr Brown: Sorry, I haven't. I **haven't had** the time.

6 *Mrs Brown:* Oh, honestly!
Have you invited the Greens?
Mr Brown: No. **We've** never **invited** the Greens to our parties.

7 *Mrs Brown:* Well, I want to invite them to this party. Go and telephone at once.

Mr Brown: Yes, dear, but I **haven't finished** the supper yet.

8 *Mrs Brown:* Then finish it. And hurry up! Men!

Questions

1 Where is Cecil?
2 Where has he been?
3 Why isn't he washing the plates?
4 Why isn't he starting the supper?
5 Why hasn't he telephoned the Blakes yet?
6 Why hasn't he invited the Greens?
7 Why doesn't he want to telephone at once?
8 What does Mrs Brown tell her husband to do?

Finished or not?

Now look at these pictures. Have the children finished yet?

1 Yes, he has.

2 No, she hasn't.

3 No, he ...

4 Yes, she ...

5 . . .

6 . . .

7 . . .

8 . . .

b Where have you been?

Mrs Carter:	Where have you been, Norman? It's after four o'clock, you know, and it'll take us four hours to Worcester.
Mr Carter:	I've just been with the manager. I've reserved the same rooms for next August. We've been so happy here.
Mrs Carter:	Oh, good. Yes, we've had a wonderful holiday.
Mr Carter:	OK, dear. Is all our luggage in the car? Right. Off we go!

Questions

1 Why is Mrs Carter worried?
2 How long will it take them to Worcester?
3 Where has Mr Carter been just now?
4 Why has he reserved the same rooms?
5 Where does Mr Carter want the luggage?

C On the motorway

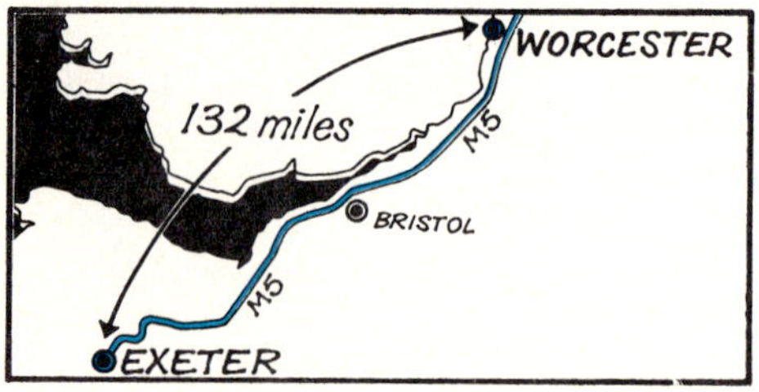

1 It is 132 miles on the M5 **motorway** from Exeter to Worcester.

2 It is **raining.**

3 The road is very **wet,** but a lot of drivers are driving too fast.

4 Near Bristol, the Carters have an awful **accident.** Mr Carter can't stop and drives into a big lorry.

5 Two **ambulances** have to take the Carters to a Bristol hospital.

6 Now the Carters have arrived at the hospital and two **doctors** are looking at Mr Carter's **broken** legs and **arm** and Mrs Carter's broken **back.**

Questions

1 How far is it from Exeter to Worcester?
2 Why are the roads wet?
3 Why mustn't the drivers drive so fast?
4 Where do the Carters have an awful accident?
5 How do the Carters go to hospital?
6 What is the matter with Mrs Carter?

d Tim in hospital

1 *Doctor:* Well, Tim, how are you feeling now? Have you had any tea?

Tim: Yes, I have, thank you. I think I'm all right.

2 *Tim:* Have you talked to my parents yet? How are they?

3 *Doctor:* Your dad has already asked about you. But I'm afraid he's very ill. He has injured his left arm and both his legs.

4 *Tim:* And my mum?

Doctor: I've just visited her. I'm afraid she has to stay here for two or three months.

5 *Tim:* Can I stay here with my parents? I want to be near them.

Doctor: Only for two or three days, Tim. You've been lucky. You can leave hospital and go to Worcester.

6 *Doctor:* I've already talked to my friend Ben Roberts. He's the warden of a children's home in Worcester. And it's near your house.

7 *Tim:* A children's home? Oh, no! I've never been in a home, and I don't want to go into a home now!

8 *Tim:* Can't you telephone my aunt? Her name is Mary Hanson and she lives in Dover. She's got a small hotel there.

Questions

1 Has Tim had any tea?
2 How is Tim feeling now?
3 How is Tim's father?
4 How long does Mrs Carter have to stay in hospital?
5 For how long can Tim stay near his parents?
6 What is Ben Roberts?
8 Who is Mary Hanson?

A boy telephones the police

Can you complete this?

This is Tom Jenkins speaking. I'm telephoning from the M5 ... The call box is ... Exeter. A ... accident has ... A ... has crashed into my father's car. And now five cars ... ... into the ... Please send some doctors and an ... I'm ... many people have ... arms and ... legs. I think one man has a broken ... It's ...! I'm afraid you'll have to reserve five beds in Exeter ... Come at once.

broken afraid to happen terrible broken back near to crash hospital lorry motorway ambulance lorry e

I'm too busy

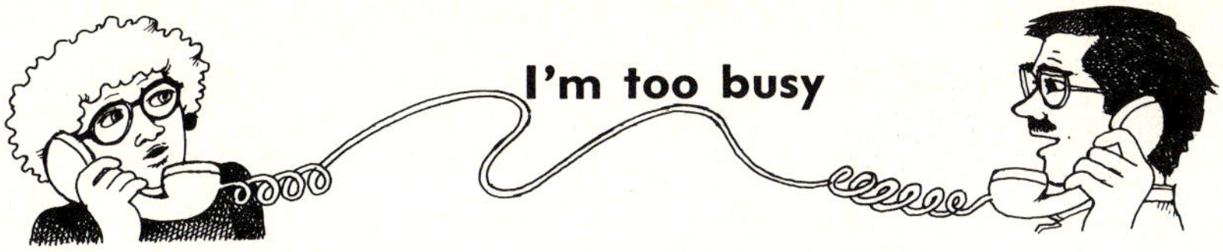

Doctor: Hello, is that Mrs Hanson? Dr Finch here. I'm telephoning from the Elizabeth II hospital in Bristol.

Mary Hanson: Yes, doctor, what's the matter? Tell me!

Doctor: Now please don't worry, Mrs Hanson. Your sister and her family have had an accident on the M5 motorway.

Mary Hanson: That's terrible. How awful! How is my sister?

Doctor: I'm afraid she's very ill. She'll have to stay here for several months. And Mr Carter, too.

Mary Hanson: And Tim? What about poor Tim?

Doctor: Oh, he's feeling fine. But, of course, he can't go to an empty house in Worcester. Have you got a bed for him?

Mary Hanson: Oh dear, oh dear! I don't want to say no, but I really can't take Tim now in August. The hotel is full and I'm too busy. He can come in October. Tell him that.

Questions

1 Where is Dr Finch telephoning from?
2 How long will Mrs Hanson's sister have to stay in hospital?
3 Why can't Tim go to his house in Worcester?
4 Can Tim go to his aunt's hotel in August?
5 When *can* he go to his aunt?

How awful!

Talk to your partner.

1 Quick, come and look!

2 What has happened?
What's the matter?

3 That ambulance has had an accident.
Sally hasn't finished her homework yet.
Mr Smith has broken his arm in the street.
A lorry has crashed into our house.
Our teacher is standing in front of our door.
Several rooms of his hotel are on fire.

4 Oh dear, oh dear.
How awful.
That's terrible.
Dear me.

Grammar Practice

1 A I've washed ...

"I've washed the car. It's clean now."

Complete these sentences.

1 **I've washed** (wash) the car. It's clean now.
2 **I've** ... (finish) my homework. I can play football now.
3 ... (pack) my suitcase. We can go now.
4 ... (talk) to Susan. She can come to the party.
5 ... (invite) Peter to the party. He can come, too.
6 ... (ask) Mum to help me. She can bake nice cakes.

1 B

Present Perfect Tense	Short Form	Negative Form
I have been	I've	I haven't
You have had	You've	You haven't
We have packed	We've	We haven't
They have cleaned	They've	They haven't
He has washed	He's	He hasn't
She has talked	She's	She hasn't
It has arrived	It's	It hasn't

In dieser Unit lernen wir eine weitere Zeitform des Verbs **(Tense)**: das PRESENT PERFECT TENSE.

Es wird immer mit 'have' gebildet:

I **have** already washed. (Ich **habe** mich schon gewaschen).
I **have** just arrived. (Ich **bin** gerade angekommen).

have/has + Verb + ed

Zwei besondere Formen merken wir uns:

I am : I have **been**
I have : I have **had**

Für die Aussprache des Verb + ed gibt es drei Möglichkeiten:

[t]		[d]		[id]	
I have	pack**ed** [t]	I have	call**ed** [d]	I have	invit**ed** [tid]
I have	ask**ed** [t]	I have	clean**ed** [d]	I have	hat**ed** [tid]
I have	finish**ed** [t]	I have	telephon**ed** [d]	I have	land**ed** [did]

Beim Schreiben beachten wir:

I hurry — I have hurried	Nach einem Konsonanten wird das **-y** zu **-ied.**
I play — I have played	Nach einem Vokal jedoch bleibt das **-y.**
I stop — I have stopped	**g, m, n, t, p** und **l** nach einem Kurzvokal werden verdoppelt.
I telephone — I have telephoned I invite — I have invited	Das stumme **-e** am Ende fällt weg.

Die Anwendung des Present Perfect Tense:

Wir dürfen es nicht mit der ähnlichen deutschen Form gleichsetzen. Wenn wir also Fehler vermeiden wollen, merken wir uns die Wörter, mit denen das Present Perfect Tense meist gekoppelt ist:

already	(schon)	I've already washed.
yet	(bis jetzt)	Have you seen him yet?
not . . . yet	(bis jetzt noch nicht)	I haven't had my breakfast yet.
just	(gerade eben)	I've just had breakfast.
ever	(jemals, überhaupt schon)	Have you ever been to France?
never	(noch nie, überhaupt noch nicht)	I've never been there.

1 C Form questions and answers

Example:

wash your hair — already/just

Have you already washed your hair?
I have just washed it.

1 telephone the Greens — yet/already
2 invite the Blacks — already/never
3 finish supper — yet/just
4 reserve the hotel-rooms — already/just
5 talk to Peter — already/just
6 clean your room — yet/just

Exercises

1 Haven't the children finished yet?

a) Look at the pictures and ask your neighbour.

Example:

You:	Look at picture No 2. Has Tom finished the letter yet?
Your friend:	No, he hasn't.

Go on.

b) Mother is in the bedroom. She is very busy. She needs help.
Father can't help. He must read his newspaper. Mother is asking him questions.

Example:

Mother:	Can Tom come and help?
Teacher:	No 1.
Father:	No, he can't. He hasn't finished with the telephone conversation.

Now you are father and mother. The teacher says the numbers.

2 Going to Land's End (Part II)

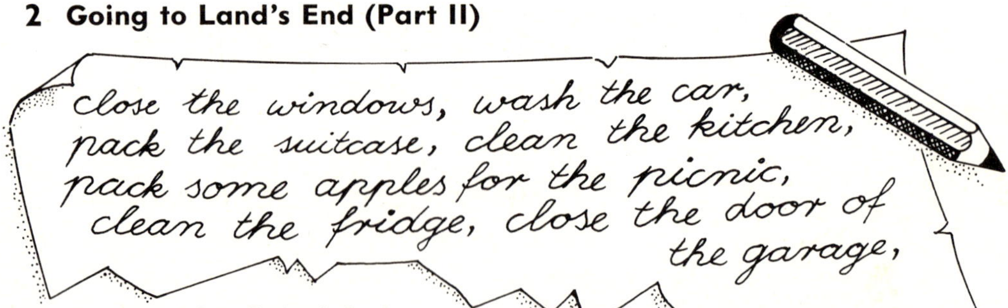

Do you remember Father's list?

The family is standing at the car.

Example:

Father:	Johnny, have you washed the car?
Johnny:	Yes, I have, Daddy.

Go on with Betty, Susan, Jerry, Tom.

3 In hospital

There are 30 beds in Tim's room. In the bed next to him there is another boy who has had an accident. They are talking about accidents, hospitals, etc.

Tim asks his neighbour some questions.

Example:

you / ever / to break your arm

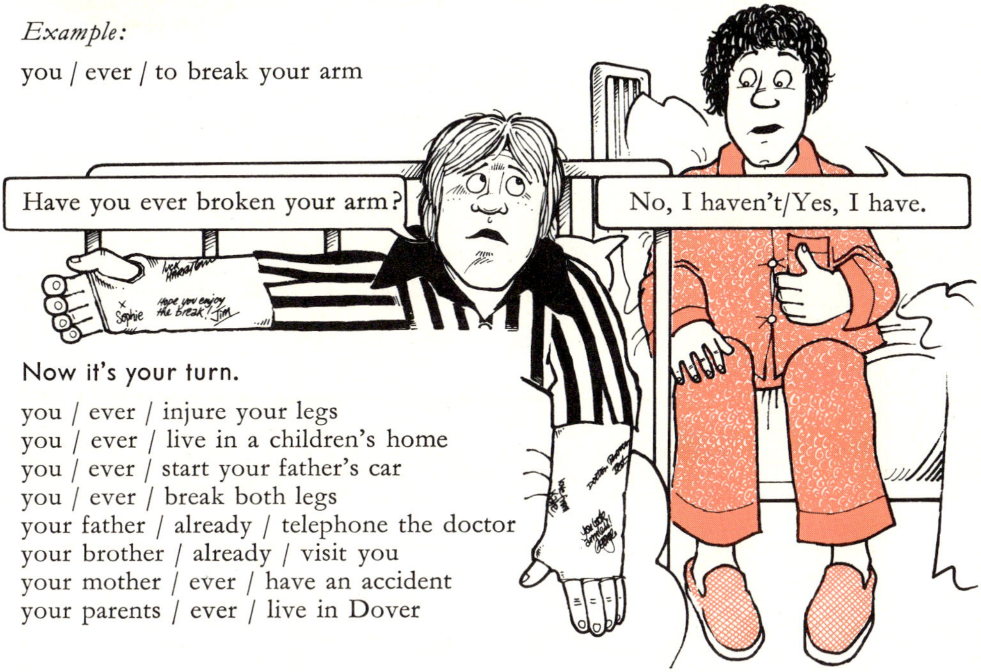

Now it's your turn.

you / ever / injure your legs
you / ever / live in a children's home
you / ever / start your father's car
you / ever / break both legs
your father / already / telephone the doctor
your brother / already / visit you
your mother / ever / have an accident
your parents / ever / live in Dover

4 Have you ever been to London?

Talk to your partner.

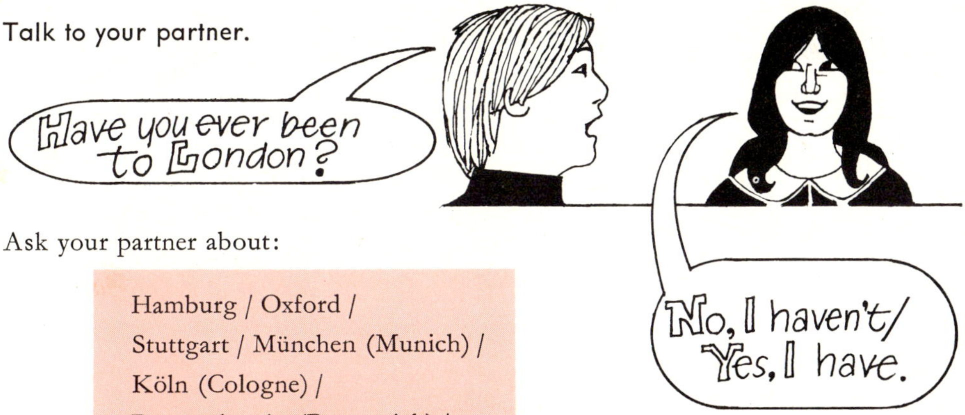

Ask your partner about:

Hamburg / Oxford /
Stuttgart / München (Munich) /
Köln (Cologne) /
Braunschweig (Brunswick) /
Hameln (Hamlin) /
New York / Worcester /

5 Plans

Example:

Tom:	What are you going to do on Saturday? Help your mother?
Peter:	No, I'm going to read that new book.

Tom:	What are you going to do on Saturday? + + +?
Peter:	No, I'm going to * * *

+ + +	* * *
Buy an alarm-clock	buy new jeans
Write to Susan	write to Fritz in Hamburg
Pack your suitcase	watch the football match on TV
Get your ticket to London	get my ticket to Worcester
Telephone your mother	write a letter to her

6 Tony loves TV

The children are watching television. Mother doesn't like that.

Example:

Mother:	Tony, have you finished your homework?
Tony:	No, I haven't. I'm going to do it in a minute.

Go on with the rest of the family:
Hazel, Tom, Jenny, Chris, Jerry, Lewis, George, Alan

wash the car
order the sausages for the party
work in the garden
rush to the baker's
invite your friends to your party
explain the new words to your sister

7 A Game

We have got a robot in the classroom. He can speak. You tell him what to do. And the robot tells you what he has done.

Bleepy, der sprechende Roboter, sagt seinem Auftraggeber stets, was er erledigt hat. Gib ihm verschiedene Aufträge, er wird sie zu deiner Zufriedenheit ausführen. Die Meldung, daß er seine Aufgabe erledigt hat, wird prompt gemacht.

Example:

You: Robot, wash your hands.
(Now he must go and wash his hands.)
Robot: Bleep — bleep — bleep —
I have just washed my hands.

Go on. Here are some more orders:

finish my homework	telephone my aunt
rush to the door	open the door
knock at the door	wash our teacher's hands

8 What have I done?

Euer Lehrer flüstert einem Schüler ins Ohr, was dieser vor der Klasse vorführen soll. Er darf dabei nichts sagen. Die Schüler versuchen, durch Fragen herauszufinden, was er vorgeführt hat. Die Bücher sind dabei geschlossen.

Example: Schüler führt Händewaschen vor.

You: Have you washed your arm?
Your friend: No, I haven't.
You: Have you washed your hands?
Your friend: Yes, I have.

Teacher: You have broken your arm.
Open a suitcase.
Knock at the door.
Clean the window.
Telephone the police.
You have broken your leg.
You are a waiter. Serve a guest.
Wash your hair.
Look at the board.
Look for a book on the floor.

Vocabulary Definitions

a

		[bleiks]	**the Blakes**
Where have you . . ., Norman?	Wo bist du **gewesen**, Cecil?	[biːn]	**been** (to be)
I haven't had the time.	Ich habe keine Zeit gehabt.		
Haven't you? Oh, . . .!	Na hör mal, **ehrlich**!	[ˈɔnistli]	*honestly*
I like the Greens. . . . them to our party.	Ich mag die Greens. **Lade** sie **ein** zu unserer Party.	[inˈvait]	**invite** (to invite)
Don't wait. You must do it . . .!	Du mußt es **sofort** tun.	[ət ˈwʌns]	**at once**

b

We must leave. It is very late and it'll . . . five hours to London.	Wir müssen los. Es ist schon sehr spät, und es **dauert** fünf Stunden bis London.	[ˈteik]	**take** (to take)
I want to . . . a room for the weekend, please.	Ich möchte bitte ein Zimmer **bestellen** für das Wochenende.	[rəˈsəːv]	**reserve** (to reserve)
And here's another suitcase.	Und hier ist noch ein Koffer.		
Is this all your . . . now?	Ist dies nun Ihr gesamtes **Gepäck**?	[ˈlʌgidʒ]	**luggage**

c

A . . . is looking at his broken leg now.	Ein **Arzt** sieht sich jetzt sein gebrochenes Bein an.	[ˈdɔktə]	*doctor*
Put your raincoat on; it is going to . . .	Zieh' deinen Regenmantel an. Es wird sicher **regnen**.	[rein]	**rain** (to rain)
Don't drive too fast; the roads are very . . .	Fahr nicht zu schnell; die Straßen sind sehr **naß**.	[wet]	**wet**
The driver can't stop his car, and there is an awful . . .	Der Fahrer kann seinen Wagen nicht anhalten, und es gibt einen furchtbaren **Unfall**.	[ˈæksidənt]	**accident**
His mother is very ill. An . . . is going to take her to hospital.	Seine Mutter ist sehr krank. Ein **Krankenwagen** wird sie ins Krankenhaus bringen.	[ˈæmbjuləns]	*ambulance*
It is a very fast road. It is the M5 . . .	Es ist die M5 **Autobahn**.	[ˈməutəwei]	**motorway**
Mr Carter can't walk. His legs are . . .	Mr Carter kann nicht gehen. Seine Beine sind **gebrochen**.	[ˈbrəukn]	**broken**
I want to go across the road, but I can't see; can I take your . . .?	Ich möchte über die Straße gehen, aber ich kann nicht sehen; kann ich Ihren **Arm** nehmen?	[aːm]	**arm**
Mrs Carter has got a broken . . .	Mrs Carter hat einen gebrochenen **Rücken**.	[bæk]	**back**

d

How are you . . . after the accident?	Wie **fühlst** du dich nach dem Unfall?	[fiːliŋ]	**feeling** (to feel)
Your mother and your father are your . . .	Deine Mutter und dein Vater sind deine **Eltern**.	[ˈpærənts]	**parents**
How are your parents?	Wie geht es deinen Eltern?		
. . . they're very ill.	Ich **fürchte**, sie sind sehr krank.	[aim əˈfreid]	**I'm afraid** (to be afraid)
My father has . . . his left arm.	Mein Vater hat seinen linken Arm **verletzt**.	[ˈindʒəd]	**injured** (to injure)

Not just one leg but ... his legs.	Nicht nur ein Bein, sondern seine **beiden** Beine.	[bəuθ]	**both**
28, 29, 30 or 31 days are one ...	28, 29, 30 oder 31 Tage sind ein **Monat**.	[mʌnθ]	**month**
		[ben ˈrɔbəts]	**Ben Roberts**
Bill has no parents; so he is in a ...	Bill hat keine Eltern; deshalb ist er in einem **Kinderheim**.	[ˈtʃildrənz ˈhəum]	**children's home**
Your mother's sister is your ...	Die Schwester deiner Mutter ist deine **Tante**.	[ɑːnt]	*aunt*
My name is Norman White and I ... in London.	Ich heiße Norman White und **wohne** in London.	[liv]	**live** (to live)

e

She'll have to stay here for ... months.	Sie wird wohl **einige** Monate hierbleiben müssen.	[ˈsevrəl]	**several**
I'm very sorry. You can't have a room. The hotel is ...	Es tut mir leid. Sie können kein Zimmer bekommen. Das Hotel ist **belegt (voll)**.	[ful]	**full**
... come and look.	Komm **schnell**! Schau mal.	[kwik]	**quick**

Be careful! There are a lot of cars and lorries on the motorway.

Unit 8

a The children's home

1 The **Queen** Elizabeth Children's Home is **in the middle of** Worcester.

2 The warden, Ben Roberts, **puts out the lights** at a quarter past ten.

3 His wife often looks very **sad**.

4 The girls' **dormitory** is on the first **floor**, and the boys' is on the second.

5 Every child has three **blankets** and its **own** small cupboard downstairs.

Questions

1 Where is the Queen Elizabeth Children's Home?
2 What does the warden do at a quarter past ten?
3 What does his wife look like very often?
4 Where is the girl's dormitory?
5 What has every child got?

Welcome to King George VI School

Can you complete this?

This is ... George VI School for boys. In this school pupils live in the school. They sleep in ... Every pupil has his ... cupboard ...
Tom Roberts is very ..., he can't live at home. His father is the ... of ... Elizabeth ... ... He wants to be at home ... of Worcester. At home the ... is ... good, but he hates the ... in the school dining-hall.

sad · meals · in the middle · own · King · Queen · food · dormitories · floor · quite · Children's Home · warden

b Tim's first meal at the home

Mary: Why are you looking so sad, Tim?
Tim: Pardon?
Mary: Is anything wrong?
Tim: No, nothing at all.
Mary: You haven't even started your meal.
You must eat something.
Don't you like it here?
You haven't talked to anyone yet.
Tim: I hate it here.
I want to go home.
I want to be with my parents.
Mary: I can understand that.
But don't worry, Tim. It'll be OK here.
You'll never be alone.

Questions

1 What does Tim look like?
2 Has Tim started his meal yet?
3 Has Tim had anything to eat yet?
4 To whom has Tim talked?
5 Why does Tim want to leave the Home?
6 Why does Mary think Tim will be OK in the Home?

Why do you look so sad?

Talk to your partner.

C A noise in the night

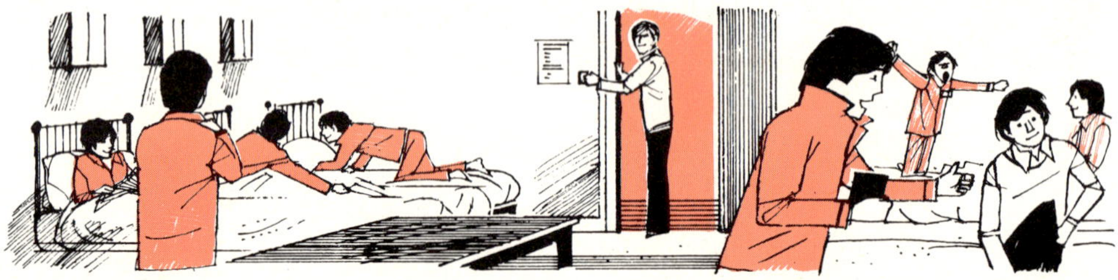

By half past nine, all the boys have finished their games and have rushed upstairs to the boys' dormitory on the second floor. Now they are lying in bed. Some boys are talking. Some are reading a paper or a book.
At a quarter past ten, Mr Roberts comes in, says 'good night', and puts the lights out. Then he returns to his room. But Tim can't sleep yet because he's worrying about his parents in Bristol. He gets up because he wants to fetch his book from his cupboard. It is quite cold. So he puts a blanket over his head. Everything is very quiet; but then Tim walks into the table in the middle of the room and wakes the other boys.

"What's that noise?" shouts a boy.
"Look, it's a ghost!" shouts another little boy and points to Tim.
"It's the White Woman of Worcester!"
"Don't be so silly. We've never had a ghost in this house," says the oldest boy and gets up. He takes his torch and puts it on.
"Take that blanket off!" he shouts. Tim throws the blanket on the floor. At that moment the warden rushes into the dormitory. He has already been to bed and is very angry. "Tell me, Tim. What are you doing there in the middle of the dormitory?" But Tim doesn't explain. "Nobody understands me," he thinks.

Questions

1 What have the boys done by half past nine?
2 What are some boys reading?
3 What does Mr Roberts do at a quarter past ten?
4 Why can't Tim sleep?
5 Why does Tim get up?
6 Why does Tim put a blanket over his head?
7 Have they ever had a ghost in the house?
8 What does the oldest boy shout?
9 Where is Tim standing at that moment?
10 Why is the warden so angry?
11 Does Tim think anybody understands him?

d Tim is late again

Mrs Roberts: You're late for breakfast again, Tim. This isn't quite good enough, you know.

Tim: I'm sorry, Mrs Roberts, but I've just had a letter from my mum. Can I go and see her tomorrow, please?

Mrs Roberts: I'm afraid I can't allow that, Tim. You have to go to school tomorrow.

Questions

1 Why does Mrs Roberts say: "This isn't quite good enough."
2 Why is Tim late for breakfast?
3 Will Mrs Roberts allow Tim to see his mother?
4 What will Tim do tomorrow?

Rules of Queen Elizabeth II Children's Home

Can you complete this?

All boys and girls ~~has~~ have to stay in their rooms ~~the~~ after the .... has put out the lights.
Don't ..... to the day rooms after half past nine.
Don't ~~jump~~ read .... or ..... in bed.
Don't pull the blankets .... your....
Don't.... books, ... or blankets on the floor.
Don't put on .... after ~~eight~~ nine o'clock.
I'll return soon!!! The ghost of the Children's Home

papers heads torches warden papers throw books return over

e Please repeat it

This is what people say when they can't understand something or when they worry about what they are saying.

I'm afraid I can't quite understand that.
I find this very difficult.
What's this thing called?
What does this phrase mean?
Please give me another example.
How do I say this word?
Please repeat that sentence.
Is this correct? Are you quite sure?
Please correct my mistakes.
How do you pronounce this word, please?

What Mr Roberts says every morning

Look at the rules and try to find out what he says. Begin with these words:

Don't ...
You mustn't ...
You must be sensible, you can't ...

Example: drink tea in bed
Mr Roberts: You mustn't drink tea in bed.

read books after nine o'clock,
put on torches on the dormitory,
wear jeans in bed,
sing in the dormitories,
sit on the tables,
throw blankets on the floor,
throw books out of the window,
have supper in the dormitory,
have transistor radios

Grammar Practice

1 A Why . . . ? Because . . .

"**Why** are you shouting?" "**Because** there is a ghost."

1 B

Can you find the answers?

1	Why are you shouting?	Because there is a ghost.
2	Why are you reading that book?	Because it . . . interesting.
3	Why are you eating those biscuits?	Because . . . hungry.
4	Why are you walking so fast?	Because . . . late.
5	Why are you dancing with Jane?	Because . . . so pretty.
6	Why are you cleaning your room?	Because . . . untidy.

Can you find more questions?

Exercises

1 A Saturday afternoon at the Children's Home

It's two o'clock on a Saturday. All the boys and girls are very busy.

a) Ask your friend questions:
You: Look at the first picture. What's Tom doing?

b) *You:* Has Tom finished that letter?
Your neighbour: Yes, he has.

Go on with these words: finish that book, wash the car, make the tea

c) It's the same every Saturday. Please ask your neighbour:
What does ... do every Saturday?
Look at picture No...

Look at the pictures and go on.

2 Have you ever had a ghost in your bedroom?

Betty and Mary are talking about the Children's Home.

Example:

Betty: Have you ever knocked at Mr Robert's door?
Mary: No, I haven't, but Johny already has.

Talk to your partner.

You: Have you ever ...?

ordered a big cake in the dining-hall /
rushed into the kitchen after half past nine /
had a ghost in your bedroom /
pulled a blanket over your head /
shaken Mr Robert's hand /
had three blankets /
been alone in your room /
allowed Tom to read your letters /
shouted in the classroom?

Your friend: No, I haven't, but ... already has.

Tom /
the teacher /
Mrs Roberts /
my father /
Jimmy /
the ghost

3 A game with the tape-recorder

Can you hear the ghost? What has he just done?

Example:

He has just knocked at the door.
...

Hasn't your teacher got a tape-recorder? Well, she/he must look at page 212 then.

Vocabulary Definitions

a

Elizabeth II is the . . of England.	Elizabeth II ist die **Königin** von England.	[kwi:n]	*queen*
I want to go to the post office, please. Then you must go through the town. The post office is . . . the town.	Ich möchte bitte zum Postamt. Dann müssen Sie durch die Stadt gehen.* Das Postamt ist in der Stadt**mitte**.	['midləv]	**in the middle of**
At a quarter past ten, the warden . . .	Um Viertel nach zehn **schaltet** der Herbergsvater **das Licht aus.**	[pu 'autts ðə 'lait]	**puts out the light** (to put out the light)
The opposite of 'happy' is . . .	Das Gegenteil von ‚glücklich' ist **‚traurig'.**	[sæd]	**sad**
In the Home the girls' . . . is on the first floor.	In dem Heim ist der **Schlafsaal** der Mädchen im ersten Stock.	['dɔ:mitri]	*dormitory*
The girls' dormitory is on the first . . . and the boys' is on the . . . floor.	Der Schlafsaal der Mädchen ist im ersten **Stock**, und der der Jungen ist im **zweiten.**	[flɔ:] ['sekənd]	**floor** **second**
It is very cold today. So the children need another . . .	Es ist sehr kalt heute. Deswegen brauchen die Kinder noch eine **Decke.**	['blænkit]	**blanket**
I can take you to the station in my car. No, thank you. I've got my . . . car there.	Ich kann Sie mit meinem Wagen zum Bahnhof fahren. Vielen Dank. Ich habe meinen **eigenen** Wagen hier.	[əun]	**own**

b

What's that? I can't hear you = . . .?	Was ist das denn? Ich kann dich nicht hören. **Wie bitte?**	['pɑ:dn]	**pardon**
Is anything wrong? — No, . . .	Nein, **überhaupt nichts.**	['nʌθiŋ ət ɔ:l]	**nothing at all**
Aren't you hungry? You must eat . . .!	Bist du nicht hungrig. Du mußt **irgend etwas** essen.	['sʌmθiŋ]	**something**
You haven't talked to Peter or Mary. You haven't talked to . . .	Du hast mit **niemandem** gesprochen.	['eniwʌn]	**anyone**
Go and visit Mary on Sunday. She is . . . in that big house. She hasn't got any friends.	Geh doch Mary am Sonntag besuchen. Sie ist **allein** in dem großen Haus. Sie hat überhaupt keine Freunde.	[ə'ləun]	**alone**

c

What's the name of the new president? You can read that in the . . .	Wie heißt der neue Präsident? Das kannst du in der **Zeitung** lesen.	['peipə]	**paper**
He comes out of his room and then he . . . to his room.	Er kommt aus seinem Zimmer und dann **geht** er wieder **zurück** in sein Zimmer.	[ri'tə:nz]	**returns** (to return)
The opposite of 'under' is . . .	Das Gegenteil von ‚unter' ist **‚über'.**	['əuvə]	**over**
Because it is cold, he puts a blanket over his . . .	Weil es kalt ist, zieht er eine Decke über seinen **Kopf.**	[hed]	**head**
It comes in the middle of the night, it is white, it is a . . .	Es kommt um Mitternacht, ist weiß, es ist ein **Geist.**	[gəust]	*ghost*

* to go — kann sowohl gehen wie auch fahren heißen.

Have you ever stayed in a youth hostel?

All the lights are out. So Tim needs a ...	Alle Lampen sind aus. Deshalb braucht Tim eine **Taschenlampe**.	[tɔːtʃ]	**torch**
I can't see. Please ... the light.	Ich kann nichts sehen. **Mach** bitte das Licht **an**.	[put'ɔn]	**put on** (to put on)
Why are you wearing that blanket? ... it ... at once!	**Nimm** sofort die Decke da **ab**!	['teik 'ɔf]	**take off** (to take off)
That's not very nice. Don't ... your chocolate on the floor!	Das ist nicht sehr nett. **Wirf** bitte deine Schokolade nicht auf den Fußboden.	[θrəu]	**throw** (to throw)
At that ... the warden rushes into the dormitory.	In dem **Moment** kommt der Herbergsvater plötzlich in den Schlafsaal.	['məumənt]	**moment**
Where is John? I don't know. Susan doesn't know. ... knows!	Wo ist John? Ich weiß es nicht, Susan weiß es nicht. **Niemand** weiß es.	['nəubɔdi]	**nobody**

d

You mustn't do that. I can't ... that.	Das darfst du nicht tun. Ich kann das nicht **zulassen**.	['əlau]	**allow** (to allow)
Now be a good boy. You must be ...	Komm, nun sei ein netter Junge. Du mußt **vernünftig** sein.	['sensibl]	**sensible**

e

What's this thing ...?	Wie **nennt** man diese Sache?	[kɔːld]	**called** (to call)
What does this ... mean?	Was bedeutet dieser **Ausdruck**?	[freiz]	**phrase**
Please give me another ...	Bitte gib mir ein weiteres **Beispiel**.	[ig'zaːmpl]	*example*
Is that ...? Is this ... right?	Ist das **richtig**? Ist dieser **Satz** richtig?	[kə'rekt] ['sentens]	*correct* **sentence**
Is this correct? Are you quite ...?	Bist du ganz **sicher**?	[ʃuə]	**sure**
Please correct my ...	Bitte korrigiere meinen **Fehler**.	[mi'steik]	**mistake**
How do you ... this word?	Wie **sprichst** du dieses Wort **aus**?	[prə'nauns]	**pronounce** (to pronounce)

9 HDYD CS 2 Textbook 42920

Unit 9

a Tim has disappeared

Mrs Roberts: Has Tim really disappeared?
Mr Roberts: I'm afraid there's been no sign of him all morning.
Mrs Roberts: Oh, dear. I haven't been very kind to him. And we haven't talked to him enough. We've treated him very badly.
Mr Roberts: I don't agree. I think we've treated him very well.
Don't worry so much, dear. He'll come back very quickly. Don't forget, he hasn't got any money.

Questions

1 For how long has Tim been away?
2 Why is Mrs Roberts worried?
3 Does her husband agree?
4 Why isn't Mr Roberts worried?
5 What mustn't his wife forget?

Peter's dog has disappeared

Can you complete this?

Peter has just ... home from school. He can't find his dog Bob. He asks his mother, but she can't tell him where Bob is. She thinks that Bob ... ...

Peter: He can't have ...
I have always ... him well.
Mother: I don't ... I think you have treated him very ...
Peter: How long has he ... away.
Mother: There has been ... ... of him all day.
Peter: I hope he'll come ... very ...
Five minutes later
Peter: Mother, come here ... Bob hasn't ...
He has been under my bed all day.

disappear, no sign, agree, back, quickly, disappear, treat, badly, disappear, be, return, quickly, disappear

Where has my little dog gone?

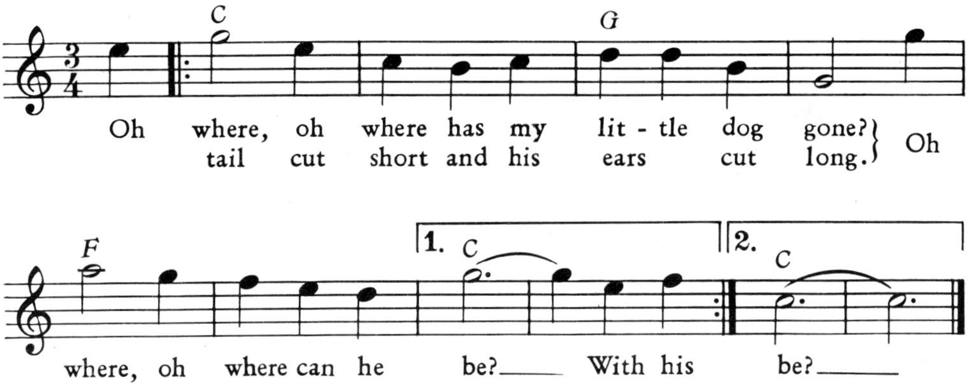

Oh where, oh where has my little dog gone?
Oh where, oh where can he be?
With his tail cut short
and his ears cut long,
oh where, oh where can he be?

b

A lift to Dover

Tim:	Could you give me a lift to the coast, please?
Lorry-driver:	I don't usually give lifts. What is a young boy like you doing here in a motorway café in the middle of the night?
Tim:	My parents are in hospital, and I want to see my aunt in Dover. Please don't leave me here.
Lorry-driver:	I don't know ...
Tim:	I'd be very grateful for your help. I can't go back to that awful children's home.
Lorry-driver:	Oh, all right. Jump in. You're lucky. I'm driving to Dover because I have to go to Gelsenkirchen tomorrow.

Questions

1 Where does Tim want to go?
2 When is Tim talking to the lorry-driver?
3 Why does Tim want to go to Dover?
4 Why is Tim lucky?

Could you do something for me?

Talk to your partner.

Example:

You:	Could you please give me a lift?
Your partner:	I don't usually do that.
You:	I'd be most grateful for your help.
Your partner:	All right, I'll give you a lift, then.

You: Could you please . . . ?

take a photograph of me and my friend / start the car for me / feed the lions / order a meal for me / close that window / do my homework for me?

Your partner: I don't usually do that.

You: I'd be most grateful for your help.

Your partner: All right, I'll . . . then.

?

You have to find out the right answer. Be careful with the words me, you, your etc.

C Tim loses his way

1 It's a **long way** from Worcester to Dover — 172 miles.

2 The lorry-driver drives very **slowly** and **carefully** — only 40 miles **per hour.**

3 So they don't **get to** Dover **before** nine o'clock.

4 They are both very hungry. So they have a large English breakfast in a café.

5 Tim **thanks** the driver **warmly**, and the driver drives off towards the boat.

6 Tim looks for his aunt's hotel in Castle Street, but he **loses his way**.

7 So he has to **ask** an old woman **the way**.

Questions

1 How far is it from Worcester to Dover?
2 How is the lorry-driver driving?
3 When do they arrive in Dover?
4 Why do they have a large breakfast?
5 How does Tim thank the driver?
6 Why doesn't Tim get to his aunt's hotel at once?
7 Who does he ask the way?

Mr Brown's way to the office

Can you complete this?

Every morning Mr Brown has to drive to his office. It's ... from his house to his office in London. He has to ... to his office ... nine o'clock. Usually he ... very slowly and carefully.
But today his car hasn't started. The taxi driver ... very quickly. But then he ... his ... He has to ... a postman the right way. He warmly ... the postman. Well, London is a ... city.

get, drive, way, thank, large, a long way, before, drive, ask, lose

d In Dover

1 *Tim:* Can you tell me how to get to Castle Street, please? Is it a long way?

Old woman: No, it isn't. You're almost there. Go down this road.

2 *Old woman:* I'll show you the way, but you'll have to walk slowly. I'm not as fast as you are!

3 *Aunt Mary:* Good heavens! Tim! What are you doing here?
Why aren't you at school in Worcester?

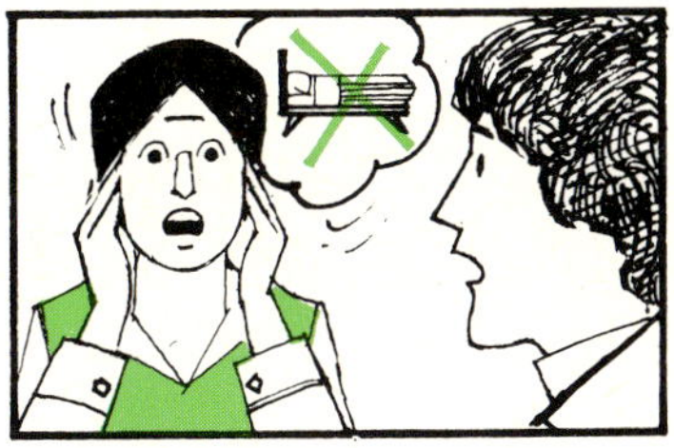

4 *Speaker:* Tim explains everything carefully, but his aunt can't give him a bed. Her hotel is quite full.

5 *Aunt Mary:* I'll have to send you back to Worcester.

Tim: I haven't got any money, Aunt Mary, and the warden will be very cross.

6 *Aunt Mary:* I'll lend you the money for the trip of course, and I'll telephone the warden.

7 *Tim:* I can't go back to Worcester today. It's 172 miles.

Aunt Mary: Oh, yes, you can. You must go as soon as possible. You can go by train.

8 *Tim:* Oh, please, Aunt Mary, let me stay.

Aunt Mary: Sorry, Tim, you're going back. But you can return for your holiday in October.

Questions

1 Where does Tim want to get to?
2 How can Tim get there?
3 Where does Tim's Aunt Mary think he must be?
4 Why can't she give him a bed?
5 Why doesn't Tim want to go back to Worcester?
6 What is Aunt Mary going to lend him?
7 Why doesn't Tim think he can go back to Worcester that day?
8 When can Tim return to Dover?

Grammar Practice

1 A slow — slowly

This is an **old** car. It is **slow**.

This is a **modern** car. It is a **fast** car. But in the city the man drives **slowly**.

That man is a **good** driver. He is driving his car **very well**.

1 B

That old car is **slow**.	Der alte Wagen ist **langsam**.
That man drives **slowly**.	Der Mann fährt **langsam**.

slow / slowly } haben die gleiche Übersetzung im Deutschen: langsam.

slow / slowly } sind im Englischen verschiedene Wörter, die im Deutschen äußerlich gleich sind

slow	ist ein Adjektiv (adjective)
slowly	ist ein Adverb (adverb)

Adjektive sagen etwas aus über die Eigenschaft eines nouns (einer Person oder Sache) — an **old** car, a **good** driver.
Adverbien beschreiben, **wie** etwas geschieht:

he drives slowly (wenn er z. B. in der Stadt immer langsam fährt)
oder: he is driving slowly (wenn er gerade jetzt langsam fährt)

Wenn wir Englisch sprechen, müssen wir zwischen Adjektiven und Adverbien unterscheiden, denn anders als im Deutschen haben sie unterschiedliche Formen. In den meisten Fällen bilden wir das Adverb, in dem wir einfach -ly an das entsprechende Adjektiv anhängen. Dabei müssen wir bei der Rechtschreibung manchmal aufpassen.

happy + ly → happ**ily**	careful + ly → carefu**lly**
angry + ly → angr**ily**	real + ly → rea**lly**

"good" hat eine besondere Form — "**well**"

1 C

Put in the right adverbs.

An old man is walking ... (slow) down the road. He is not feeling ... (good) and he is very tired. A car is coming ... (quick) down the road. The driver is not driving very ... (careful). There is almost an accident.
The car ... (quick) disappears, but the driver of the next car is giving the old man a lift. And the old man thanks him ... (warm).

Exercises

1 My dad is a policeman

Talk to your partner.

Example:

Partner: I'm awfully worried. My dad is a ... and he hasn't come home yet.
You: You don't have to worry. He usually ... very carefully.

work in the kitchen /
take children across the road /
drive /
watch the traffic /
prepare the meals

Now look at the pictures and go on.

2 He often needs small change

Do you know where to put the adverb?

Examples:

1 Carsten **has telephoned** Enquiries. (never)
Carsten **has** *never* **telephoned** Enquiries.

2 Michael **is telephoning** Enquiries. (still)
Michael **is** *still* **telephoning** Enquiries.

3 Michael **can telephone** his father. (always)
Michael **can** *always* **telephone** his father.

4 Michael **telephones** Enquiries. (often)
Michael *often* **telephones** Enquiries.

5 Michael **needs** small change. (usually)
Michael *usually* **needs** small change.

Now go on:

1 Mary telephones her mother (often)
2 That woman has washed a car (never)
3 Lulu is singing a song (still)
4 Tom has started that letter (already)
5 The policeman watches the traffic (usually)
6 Mary goes to Hamburg in her holidays (usually)
7 He has been to New York (often)
8 He can go there next week (still)
9 Tom has been to Oxford (never)
10 Susan cooks Irish stew on Sundays (always)

3 Tom is awfully sorry

Make as many sentences as you can.

Tom Susan The tea The meal Mary	is must be	terribly awfully very	cold hot bad kind sorry

4 Tim's Aunt

Now it's nine o'clock in the evening. Tim's aunt asks him where he has been all day long. Tim tells her everything about the lorry and his day in Dover.

Look at the map.

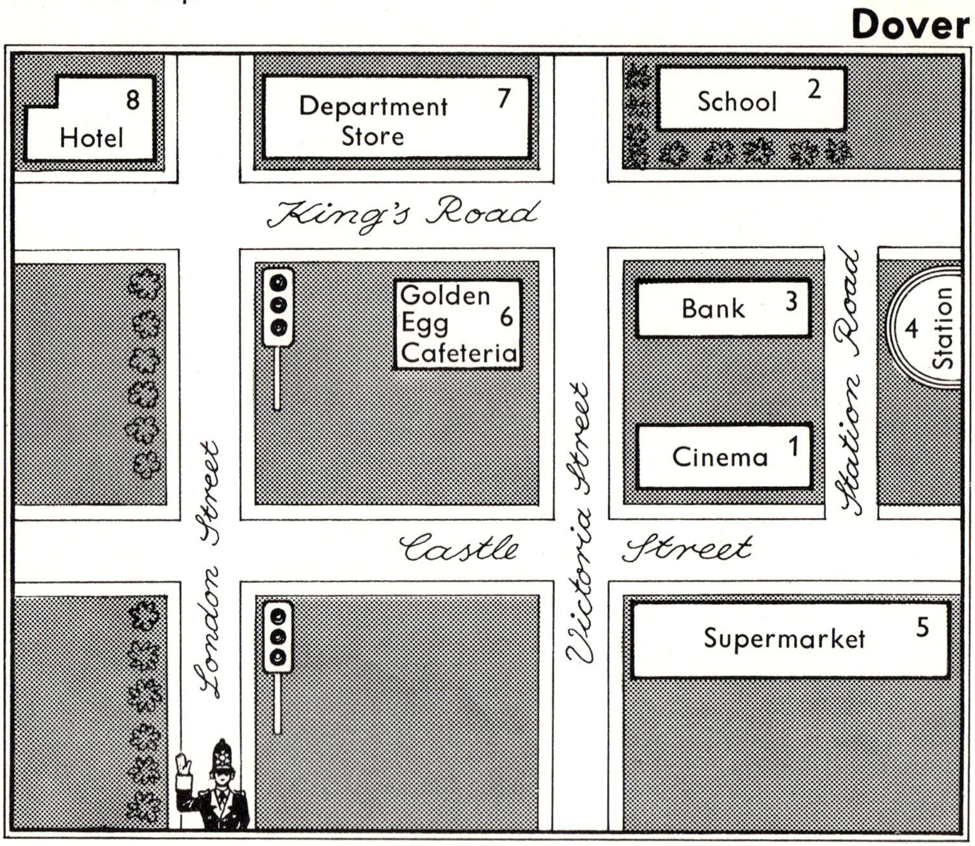

a)

Example:

Aunt: Where have you been all day long?
Tim: Oh, I've been to the department store in King's Road.

Now you are the aunt and your partner is Tim. Go on. Use these words.

No 1 (at)	No 5 (in)
No 2 (at)	No 6 (at)
No 3 (at)	No 7 (at)
No 4 (at)	No 8 (in)

b) Now she is asking him what he is going to do tomorrow.

Look at the map again.

Example:

Aunt: What are you going to do tomorrow?
Tim: I'm going to buy a book at the department store.

Go on. Now you are Tim and your partner is the aunt.

buy a book at ... (No 7) ...
have dinner at ... (No 6) ...
get some money at ... (No 3) ...
see a film at ... (No 1) ...
ask for a room at ... (No 8) ...
buy a ticket at ... (No 4) ...
buy some chocolate at ... (No 5) ...

c) In Dover there are a lot of German and French people.
They ask the policeman:

How can I get to ..., please?
Can you tell me the way to ...?

The policeman answers:

Go to the ...
Go down/up ...
Turn left/right at ...
Turn left/right into ... Street/Road
Then go straight on until you reach ...
The ... is on the left/right

5 The adverb game

Example:

You: Tim is a bad writer. How does he write?
Member of the other team: Tim writes badly.

If he can answer within five seconds he'll get a point.

Go on:

Tim is a bad singer.
Tim is a bad driver.
Tim is a quick runner.
Tom is a slow runner.
Susan is a bad writer.
Mr Brown is a careful driver.
Jimmy is a good football player.
Mr Cartwright is an awful speaker.

Vocabulary Definitions

a

We can't find Tim. He has ...	Wir können Tim nicht finden. Er ist **verschwunden**.	[disə'piəd]	**disappeared** (to disappear)
Where is Tim? I'm afraid there's ... him.	Wo ist Tim? Leider ist **nichts von** ihm **zu sehen**.	['sainəv]	**no sign of**
There's been no sign of him ...	Man hat ihn den **ganzen Morgen** nicht gesehen.	[ɔ:l 'mɔ:niŋ]	**all morning**
I haven't been very nice. I haven't been ... to him.	Ich bin nicht **nett** zu ihm gewesen.	[kaind]	**kind**
You have not been very kind to him: You have not ... him very kindly.	Du warst nicht sehr freundlich zu ihm: Du hast ihn nicht sehr freundlich **behandelt**.	['tri:tid]	**treated** (to treat)
We've treated him very ...	Wir haben ihn sehr **schlecht** behandelt.	['bædli]	**badly**
The opposite of 'good' is ...	Das Gegenteil von ‚gut' (Adjektiv) ist **‚schlecht'**.	[bæd]	**bad**
The opposite of 'badly' is ...	Das Gegenteil von ‚schlecht' (Adverb) ist **‚gut'**.	[wel]	**well**
Hurry up! Come back ...!	Mach zu! Komm **schnell** zurück.	['kwikli]	**quickly**

b

Do you think you can help me? ... you help me?	Meinst du, du kannst mir helfen? **Könntest** du mir helfen?	[kud]	**could**
Can you give me ... to the coast?	Können Sie mich **mitnehmen** bis zur Küste?	[lift]	**lift**
Do you often get up at seven? Do you ... get up at seven?	Stehst du oft um sieben auf? Stehst du **gewöhnlich** um sieben auf?	['ju:ʒuəli]	**usually**
You can get a nice cup of coffee and a cake at the ...	Du kannst eine schöne Tasse Kaffee und Kuchen im **Café** bekommen.	[kæ'fei]	*café*
I need help and I'd be very ... for it.	Ich brauche Hilfe und würde sehr **dankbar** dafür sein.	['greitful]	**grateful**

c

		['dəuvə]	**Dover**
It's a ... from Hamburg to Stuttgart.	Es ist ein **weiter Weg** von Hamburg nach Stuttgart.	['lɔŋ 'wei]	**long way**
The opposite of 'quickly' is ...	Das Gegenteil von ‚schnell' ist **‚langsam'**.	['sləuli]	**slowly**
Please don't drive so fast. Drive ...	Fahr bitte nicht so schnell. Fahr **vorsichtig**.	['kɛəfli]	**carefully**
In this car he can drive 80 miles in one hour. He drives 80 miles ...	Mit diesem Auto kann er 130 km **in einer Stunde fahren**. Er fährt 130 Stundenkilometer. (80 miles = ca. 130 km)	[pər'auə]	**per hour**
Can I ... Dover on this road?	**Komme** ich **nach** Dover auf dieser Straße?	['getə]	**get to** (to get to)
Can I get to Dover ... 9 o'clock?	Kann ich Dover noch **vor** 9 Uhr erreichen?	[bi'fɔ:]	**before**
Say 'thank you very much' to the driver. You must ... him.	Sag dem Fahrer ein ‚Dankeschön'. Du mußt dich bei ihm **bedanken**.	[θæŋk]	**thank**
Tim thanks the driver very much. He thanks him ...	Tim bedankt sich bei dem Fahrer. Er bedankt sich **herzlich**.	['wɔ:mli]	**warmly**

He goes the wrong way. He ... his way.	Er fährt die falsche Strecke. Er **verfährt** sich.	[luːziz]	**loses** (to lose one's way)
You must ... someone ...	Du mußt jemanden **nach dem Weg fragen**.	[ˈaːsk ðə ˈwei]	**ask the way** (to ask the way)

d

		[ˈkaːsl ˈstriːt]	**Castle Street**
You are not there yet, but it is not far. You are ... there.	Du bist noch nicht da, aber es ist nicht mehr weit. Du bist **beinahe** da.	[ˈɔːlməust]	**almost**
Go ... this road.	Fahren Sie auf dieser Straße **weiter**.	[dəun]	**down**
I'll show you where it is: I'll ... you ...	Ich werde Ihnen zeigen, wo es ist:	[wei]	**the way**
	Ich werde Ihnen **den Weg zeigen**. zeigen.	[ˈʃəu ðə ˈwei]	**show the way** (to show someone the way)
You must return to Worcester: I'll ... to Worcester.	Du mußt nach Worcester zurückfahren. Ich werde **dich zurückschicken** nach Worcester.	[ˈsend ju ˈbæk]	**send you back** (to send someone back)
What? You have no money? OK. I'll ... you the money.	Was? Du hast kein Geld (bei dir)? Gut. Ich werde dir das Geld **leihen**.	[lend]	**lend** (to lend)
There is not a lot of time. You must go now. You must go ...	Es bleibt nicht viel Zeit. Du mußt jetzt los. Du mußt **so bald wie möglich** fahren.	[əˈsuːnəs ˈpɔsiblə]	**as soon as possible**
Go to the station and go ...	Geh zum Bahnhof und fahr **mit dem Zug**.	[bai ˈtrein]	**by train**
Oh, please, Aunt Mary, ... me stay.	Ach bitte, Tante Mary, **laß** mich bleiben.	[let]	**let** (to let)
		[ɔkˈtəubə]	**October**

Exercise 4

I'm going to buy a ...	Ich werde eine **Fahrkarte** kaufen.	[ˈtikit]	*ticket*

I'm going back to Worcester by train.

Revision Unit II

A new group

On August 4th, Tim is back in Worcester, and on Saturday there is a big dance at Nunnery Wood School. Tim is there, too. And he is not alone. He is happier now because he has got a new friend at the Children's Home — Betty Everton, a very pretty girl with fair hair and brown eyes. He has invited her to the dance and they are looking very happy. But the head girl, Carol, is very worried.

Head girl: This is terrible. I just don't know what to do.
Betty: What's the matter, Carol?
Head girl: The 'Angry Manchester Six' haven't arrived.
Tim: What are we going to do?
We can't dance without a group. Have you telephoned their hotel?
Head girl: Yes, I have. There's no sign of them there or in the school.
We've searched everywhere.
Betty: I know, we'll serve the children the ham rolls now.
Tim: Yes, and I'll go and fetch the record-player. We'll start with some records.
Head girl: We can't do that. The record-player is broken, I'm afraid.
Tim: Wait a moment. I've got an idea — why don't you ask Mr Parrott, the music teacher? He can play the piano for us.
Betty: Don't be silly, Jimmy. He'll play Tangos.
I have a better idea. Let's ask our German friends from Hamburg.
Head girl: You're quite right, Betty. They can play for us. They're very good.
Where are they now?
Tim: They're drinking lemonade with Brian and Eileen over there. I'll fetch them. We must start as soon as possible.

Ten minutes later

Head girl: Listen for a minute, please. Our group from Manchester hasn't arrived. I've just had the news: Their van has had an accident on the motorway. But our guests from Hamburg will play for us this evening. Their group is called 'The Five Happy Hamburgers' and they're going to start with a great number:
The Lion's Rock

Questions

1 When is Tim back in Worcester?
2 Where are they having the big dance?
3 Describe Betty Everton, please.
4 Why does the head girl look so worried?
5 What does Betty want to do?
6 Why can't Tim play some records?
7 What's wrong with Mr Parrot's music?
8 What is Betty's idea?
9 Why hasn't the group from Manchester arrived?
10 What are the Hamburgers going to play first?

Listen! That's a hot number. Let's do this . . .	Hör mal. Das ist ein schneller Titel. Laß uns den **tanzen.**	[dɑːns]	**dance** (to dance)
		[ˈtæŋgəu]	**tango**
Can you play the . . .?	Kannst du **Klavier** spielen?	[piˈænəu]	*piano*
		[ˈmæntʃistə]	**Manchester**
		[ˈlaiənz ˈrɔk]	**Lion's Rock**

10 HDYD CS 2 Textbook 42920

Exercises

1 Who is he?

A new boy has just arrived in the Children's Home. Ronald has just had his first meal in the dining-hall. He is talking to Jimmy.

Example:

Ron:	Who is that man over there? 1
Jimmy:	That's Mr Roberts. 2
Ron:	Who is he? 3
Jimmy:	Don't you know him? He's the warden here. 4 3 5

Go on with:

1 that girl who says: "Listen for a minute, please!" / those boys with the guitars / the girl here / that boy with the blanket / those boys on the stage
2 Carol / "The Angry Manchester Six" / Betty / the Dark Man of Worcester / The Five Happy Hamburgers
3 he/she/they
4 him/her/them
5 headgirl / band for our dance / my new friend / the ghost of the school / our guests from Germany

2 Ronald in the dormitory

Example:

Ron: Is this **our** dormitory?
Jim: No, that is the younger boys' dormitory. We mustn't go into **their** room.

Can you complete this conversation?
Fill in my, your, his, her, our, your, their

Ron: Is this ... bed?
Jim: No, that's Tom's bed. You mustn't put ... suitcase on ... bed. Look, this is ... bed.
Ron: Is that my cupboard over there?
Jim: No, that's Michael's cupboard. You mustn't put ... books in ... cupboard. Look this is ... cupboard.

Ron: Is that our washroom?
Jim: No, that's the girl's washroom. We mustn't wash in ... washroom. Look, ... washroom is over there.
Ron: Is that the dining-hall for all the boys and girls?
Jim: Yes, you are right. This is ... dining-hall. But you mustn't sit on this chair. It's Mr Robert's chair. Don't ever sit on ... chair.
Ron: Can I sit here?
Jim: No, I'm sorry you can't. That is Mrs Robert's chair. Don't ever sit on ... chair.
Ron: Can I sit at ... table next to you, then?
Jim: Oh, yes of course, we can put another chair at ... table.
Ron: Thank you so much. You are my best friend here.

3 The band hasn't arrived yet!

The boys and girls don't know what to do. But Carol has an idea. And so do Tom and Betty and Tim and ...
Now they are talking about their ideas.

Example:

Jimmy: What are we going to do?
Headgirl: I've got an idea.
Let's ask Mr Parrot. He can play the piano.
Susan: I have a better idea. Let's ask our German friends. They can sing and play the guitar.

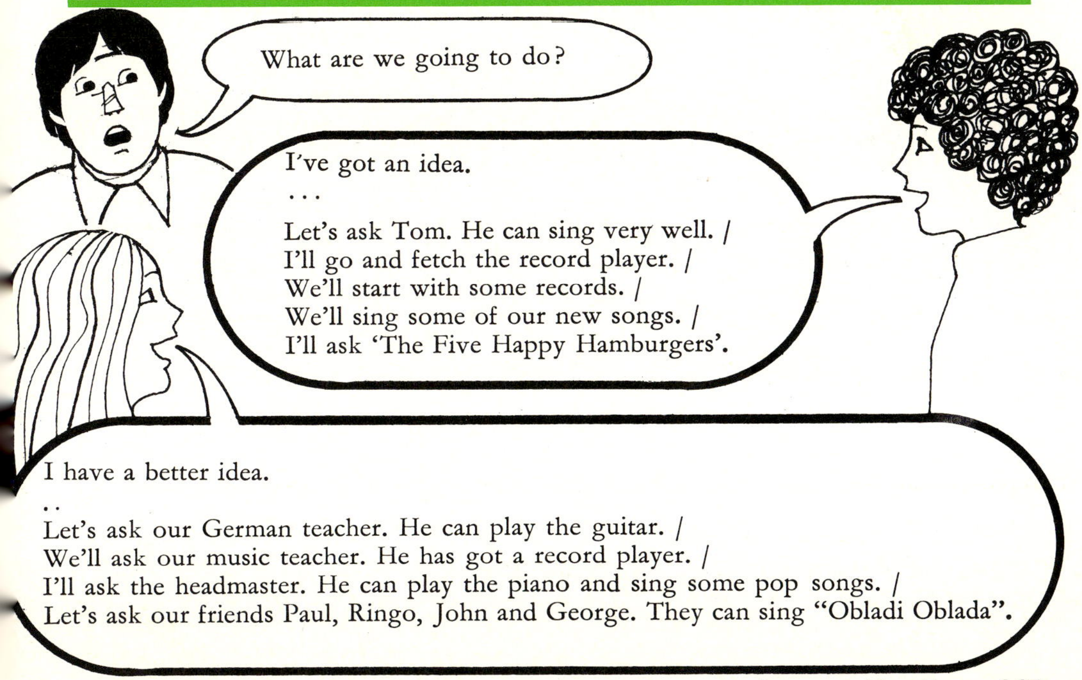

4 Can you ask questions?

Example:

Jimmy warmly thanks the driver in Dover
1 2 3 4

1 Who thanks the driver?
2 How does Jimmy thank the driver?
3 What does Jimmy do?
4 Where does Jimmy thank the driver?

Dies ist ein Frage- und Antwortspiel in der Klasse. Bildet zwei Mannschaften. Jede Mannschaft wählt sich einen passenden Namen. (Lions, tigers, elephants, birds, . . .). Ein Schüler aus der Mannschaft der "lions" fragt einen "tiger" die erste Frage: "Who thanks the driver?" Der "tiger" antwortet: „Jimmy does" und stellt die zweite Frage: "How does Jimmy thank the driver?" Für jede richtige Frage gibt es einen Punkt. Kann der "tiger" die zweite Frage nicht stellen, so ruft der Lehrer einen Schüler der Gruppe "lions" auf.

1 Tom is drinking lemonade with Brian over there.
1 2 3 4

2 Their van has had an accident on the motorway.
1 2 3

3 The 'Five Happy Hamburgers' are going to start with the "Lion's Rock" soon.
1 2 3 4

4 Tim and Betty have had a good time at the dance.
1 2 3

5 Brenda often forgets her homework on Wednesdays.
1 2 3 4

6 Tim never reads in bed.
1 2 3 4

5 Oh these children!

Mr and Mrs Roberts are talking about the children. But they never agree. Fill in the correct form of these words: quick, good, nice, quiet, bad, slow, sad, happy, angry.

Example:

Mr Roberts: I think we have treated Jim very . . .
Mrs Roberts: Oh, no! I think we have treated him . . .

Mr Roberts: I think we have treated Tim very **badly**.
Mrs Roberts: Oh, no! I think we have treated him **well**.

Go on:

Mrs Roberts: Carol has cleaned the kitchen very . . .
Mr Roberts: Oh, no! I think she usually cleans it very . . .

Mrs Roberts: Tom is doing his homework ... again.
Mr Roberts: Really? I think he does it ... every day.

Mrs Roberts: Look at Brenda. She often does her work ...
Mr Roberts: Really? I think she does it ... every day.

Mrs Roberts: Listen, Ron is shouting again.
Mr Roberts: That's right, but usually he talks ...

Mrs Roberts: Look at John on his bike. He is cycling very ... today.
Mr Roberts: Yes, but usually he cycles very ...

Mrs Roberts: Listen! Betty is singing very ...
Mr Robert: That's right, dear, but usually she sings very ...

6 The party

All the boys and girls like the music and the party. There is a long table with many things to eat and drink.

a) Carol and Tom are talking about the things on the table.

Example:

Carol: I like this tea. It's very good.
Tom: Yes, but I like this fruit juice better.

Look at the picture and go on.

b) Susan is standing behind the table. She can see the things on the table but she cannot see the prices. She asks Tom and Carol.

Example:
Susan: Tom, how much are the oranges?
Tom: They are ...p each.
Look at the picture and go on.

c) Now sell these things to your friends.

Example:
Your friend: Can I have two oranges, please? How much are they?
You: Can't you see? They are 20p each.

Look at the picture on page 149. There are a lot of things that you want to buy. Go on.

7 A game with the tape-recorder

Example:
Tape: Compare Tom and John. What about their age?
Pupil: 'Tom is older than John' *or* 'John is younger than Tom.'

Now it's your turn.
Can you answer all the questions? Well, look at page 212.

Unit 10

a On the car ferry Prince Hamlet

Carol Lamb and fifteen other children from the Worcester school are going to Hamburg today. They are visiting their Hamburg pen-friends for three weeks. They are going on the **car ferry** Prince Hamlet from Harwich. The boat leaves Harwich at one o'clock and arrives in Hamburg at nine o'clock the **next morning.**

Questions

1 What are the fifteen children doing today?
2 For how long are they going?
3 How are they going to Hamburg?
4 When does the boat leave?
5 When will the children arrive?

b Carol is packing her suitcase

1 *Mother:* Don't leave your ticket on the table, Carol.
Carol: Oh, dear. You're right. **I have left** it on the table.

2 *Carol:* Where is my white dress, Mum? I can't see it here.
Mother: I know, **I've seen** it. It's on my bed.

3 *Mother:* Have you got enough sandwiches, dear? Perhaps you can buy some at the station?
Carol: No, thanks, **I've bought** a meat-pie. That's enough.

4 *Mother:* You must tell me, dear — have you got enough money?
Carol: **I've told** you again and again. Yes, thank you, more than enough, Mum.

5 *Carol:* Where's my passport? Please give me my passport. There isn't a lot of time.
Mother: I don't know. What's the matter with you? **I've** just **given** you your passport!

6 *Carol:* Is Dad coming home before I go?
Mother: He **has** already **come**. He's waiting for you in the car.

Questions

1 What has Carol done with the ticket?
2 What has her mother seen on her bed?
3 Why doesn't Carol want any sandwiches?
4 What has Carol told her mother again and again?
5 Why can't her mother give Carol her passport?
6 Who has already come?

I've already seen that film

Talk to your neighbour.

Example:

You: Are you going to buy some meat-pies this afternoon?
Your friend: No, I've already bought them.

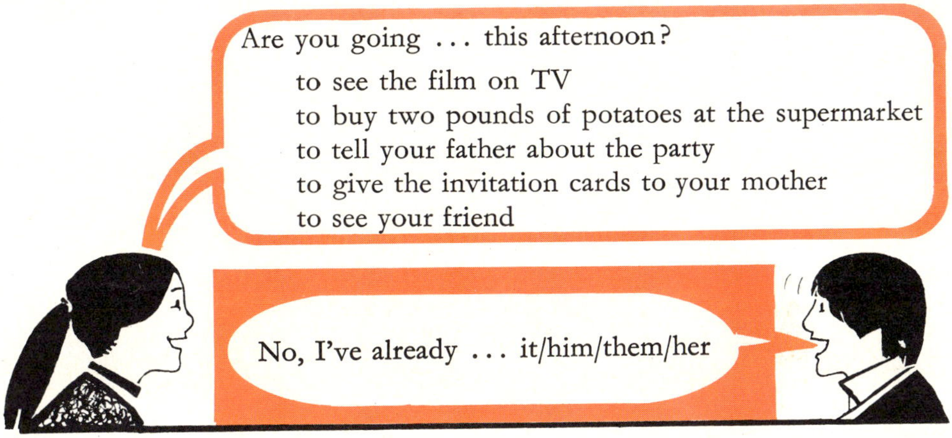

C Don't sleep on the floor!

David: Have you seen Carol, Eileen?
Eileen: Yes, I've just come from her. She's given me this ticket for a bed.
David: Has she bought tickets for us all?
Eileen: I don't think so.
David: Then I must go and get a ticket, too.
Eileen: You're too late, I'm afraid. Bill has told me the boat is full today.
David: I'll go now. I don't want to sleep on the floor.
Eileen: Well, you can always stay in the cafeteria and put your head on a table.
David: Thank you very much!

Questions

1 Has Eileen seen Carol?
2 What has Carol given her?
3 Has Carol bought tickets for all of them?
4 Why can't David get a ticket?
5 What can David do in the cafeteria?
6 Does David like that idea?

At the station

Can you complete this?

Eileen has just ... Carol. She has just ... from the station. She has ... tickets for them all. Carol has ... her these tickets. Bill has ... her: "The boat is full today".

come, seen, given, bought, told

d On the way to Hamburg

1 Eileen has just **eaten** two rolls.

2 It is half past ten, and everyone goes to his or her **cabin**.

3 Mr King, their teacher, is also **tired** now.

4 The **twins,** Peggy and Pat, have got hot and cold water in their cabin and two pieces of **soap.**

5 There is a **strong** wind. Carol has just **fallen** out of bed.

6 Now the boat has **reached** Hamburg.

7 There is a big **crowd** on deck.

Questions

1 What has Eileen just done?
2 What does everyone do at half past ten?
3 Why is Mr King also going to bed?
4 Is Peggy much older than Pat?
5 Why has Carol fallen out of bed?
6 Which city has the boat just reached?
7 How many people are there on deck?

On the ferry

Can you complete this?

The boys and girls are going to sleep in ... They are very ... because they have ... a big dinner. In the morning Peggy and Pat get up. They are ... After breakfast they go on ... They can't walk because there is a ... A man has just ... down. A big ... is standing round him. The doctor has ... him some medicine. Now he is OK. At 9 o'clock the ferry will ... Hamburg.

reach, tired, crowd, give, twins, fall, cabins, eat, deck, strong wind

A game with the tape-recorder

Listen to this. What has happened?

Hört euch die Geräusche vom Tonband an und versucht herauszufinden, was passiert ist.

Example:

Tape: What has happened to Peter?
You: Peter has fallen out of bed.

Has your teacher got a tape-recorder? Well she must look at page 212 then.

e A girl in the water

Mr King, the teacher of the Worcester boys and girls, is having his breakfast in the cafeteria of the Prince Hamlet. He has already eaten two eggs, bacon and three rolls with marmalade and he has just bought his third cup of coffee.
Now Carol, the head girl, is coming to his table. She is very anxious.
"Mr King, one of the twins is missing. We can't find Pat anywhere. And we'll reach Hamburg soon."
"Have you searched everywhere?" Mr King asks her.
"Yes, I have," Carol replies. "I've looked in all the cabins and I've asked everyone."
"Good heavens, Carol, you don't mean she's fallen into the water?" Mr King shouts and runs out of the cafeteria. "Stop the boat, stop the boat! One of my girls is missing!" he shouts.
A big crowd is now standing next to Mr King on deck and is looking into the water of the Elbe. And then a girl with red hair looks out of a lifeboat and asks, "Excuse me, has there been an accident? How exciting!"
"Pat!" shouts Carol, "what are you doing there?"
"I'm sunbathing," Pat replies. "These lifeboats are very useful for that."

Questions

1 What is Mr King doing in the cafeteria?
2 What has Mr King just bought?
3 Why is the head girl very anxious?
4 Where has Carol searched?
5 Where does Mr King think Pat is?
6 Who is standing next to Mr King on deck?
7 Who looks out of the boat?
8 What is she doing in the boat?

The missing ball-point

Tom has bought an expensive ball-point for his German friend Dieter. But now he can't find it. So he asks Carol.

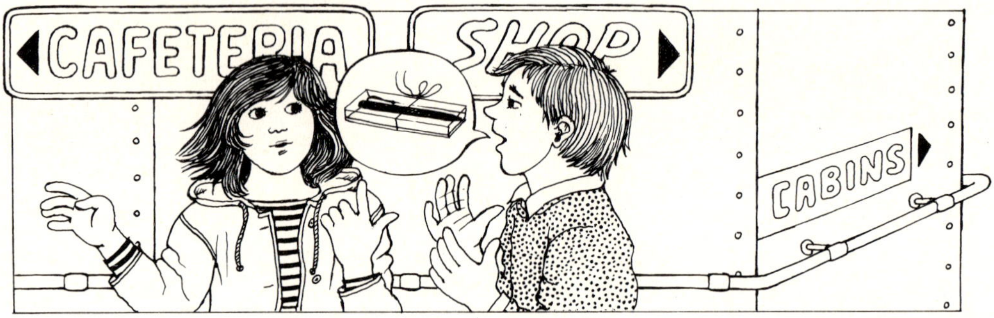

Example:

Tom: **Have you seen** my new ball-point? I can't find it anywhere.
Carol: **No, I haven't.**

Complete this conversation.

Carol: (you/search) ... everywhere?	*Tom:* Yes, ...
Carol: (you/ask) ... Mr King?	*Tom:* No, ...
Carol: (you/look) ... in your cabin?	*Tom:* Yes, ...
Carol: (you/give) ... it to a friend?	*Tom:* No, ...
Carol: (you/leave) ... it in the cafeteria?	*Tom:* No, ...
Carol: (you/see) ... it since breakfast?	*Tom:* No, ...
Carol: (you/be) ... on deck with it?	*Tom:* I don't know.
Carol: (you/leave) ... it in the shop?	*Tom:* No, ...

Can you complete this?

Carol says: This is too bad. The pen must have fallen into the water. Look, Linda is just coming round that corner. Perhaps she ... your pen. Linda shouts: Look, what I've got. It's a very expensive ball-point. Someone ... it in the cafeteria. Carol: Oh, how lucky you are, Tom. Carol laughs: "You ... too anxious about your pen. Now let's get our suitcases ready. We'll be in Hamburg soon.

(be, see, leave)

Grammar Practice

1 A Present Perfect Tense of Irregular Verbs

"Look, our ferry **has** already **left**."

I you we they	+ have	left seen bought told
he she it	+ has	given come eaten

1 B Regular Verbs

In Unit 7 haben wir gelernt, daß man an viele englische Verben -ed anhängt, um die Form für das Present Perfect zu erhalten:

finish — I have just finish**ed** my breakfast

telephone — She has already telephon**ed** the Bakers.
Diese Verben heißen Regular Verbs = regelmäßige Verben, denn sie werden alle auf die gleiche Art verändert: durch Anhängen der Silbe -ed.

Irregular Verbs

Eine Reihe anderer Verben hat dafür besondere Formen, die wir lernen müssen:

leave	— The ferry **has** already **left.**
	— I **have left** my ticket on the table.
see	— **Have** you **seen** my ticket?
buy	— I **have bought** a meat-pie.
tell	— She **has told** me again and again.
give	— He **has** just **given** me the passport.
come	— Dad **has** already **come** home.
eat	— I **have** already **eaten.**
fall	— A man **has** just **fallen** down.

Diese Verben heißen Irregular Verbs = unregelmäßige Verben, weil jedes seine besondere Form hat.
Die unregelmäßigen Verben sind in einer Liste zusammengestellt und nach dem Alphabet geordnet in der List of Irregular Verbs (Seite 216). Für das Present Perfect Tense brauchen wir aus der Liste die Wörter der dritten Spalte (Part 3).
Die Anwendung des Present Perfect Tense mit den unregelmäßigen Verben ist die gleiche wie mit den regelmäßigen (Unit 7).

1 C What they have just done?

Make some sentences like this:

Brian / buy a ticket	Brian has just bought a ticket.
Brian / leave the ticket on the table	Brian has ...
Carol / see the ticket	Carol ...
Carol / tell Brian about the ticket	...
Carol / give Brian the ticket	...
Their teacher / come	...
The ferry / leave	...
A man / fall into the water	...
... / eat ...	...
... / see ...	...
... / buy ...	...
... / ...	...

Exercises

1 Have you seen my pen?

You have lost your new pen. Your friend wants to help you. Make up a conversation.

Have you seen my new pen?
... my book /
... Peter's notebook /
... Tom's English book /
... my dog /
... my left shoe /
... my bag?

No, I haven't.
Have you looked under your bed?
... in the kitchen /
... in the cupboard?
... in the dormitory /
... on the table /
... behind the board?

Have you asked / Have you given it to — your teacher / father / mother / your sister / Betty?

Now act this conversation!

2 This soup is awful!

You don't like it. What do you say when you complain?

Ein Gast beschwert sich beim Steward.

Act this conversation:

Tourist:	This	cabin food soup ferry music cafeteria	is	awful cold too quiet late too small too fast
Tourist:	I'd like to speak to the			manager captain head waiter

Steward: I can't understand this. Everyone likes our ...
Tourist: Well, I don't. Please go and get the ...
Steward: At once, sir. I'm very sorry.

3 What are your plans for tomorrow?

Mr King wants to know what the boys and girls are going to do in Hamburg.

Example:

Mr King: Tom, what are your plans for tomorrow?
Tom: I'm going to visit the Reeperbahn.

Talk to your partner.

... to telephone my parents
... to watch German TV
... to see a film
... to sleep all day long
... to go shopping
... to go on a trip to Lübeck
... to read this book
... to write letters

11 HDYD CS 2 Textbook 42920

4 Comprehension Exercise

A letter from the Prince Hamlet

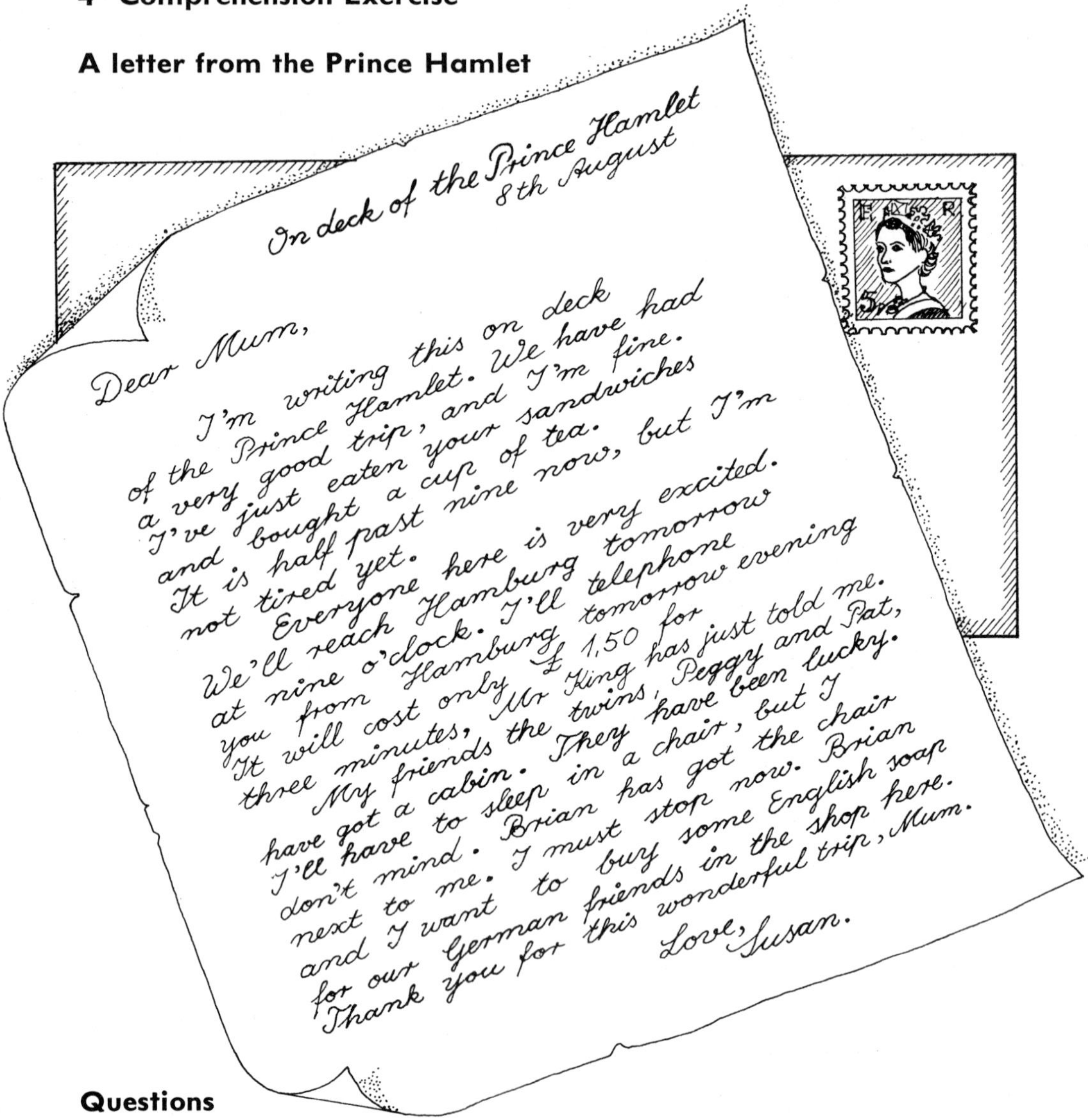

On deck of the Prince Hamlet
8th August

Dear Mum,

I'm writing this on deck of the Prince Hamlet. We have had a very good trip, and I'm fine. I've just eaten your sandwiches and bought a cup of tea. It is half past nine now, but I'm not tired yet.

Everyone here is very excited. We'll reach Hamburg tomorrow at nine o'clock. I'll telephone you from Hamburg tomorrow evening. It will cost only £1,50 for three minutes, Mr King has just told me.

My friends the twins, Peggy and Pat, have got a cabin. They have been lucky. I'll have to sleep in a chair, but I don't mind. Brian has got the chair next to me. I must stop now. Brian and I want to buy some English soap for our German friends in the shop here. Thank you for this wonderful trip, Mum.

Love, Susan.

Questions

1 Where is Susan writing this letter?
2 What has Susan just bought?
3 Why is Susan not in bed yet?
4 When will the boat reach Hamburg?
5 When will Susan telephone her mother?
6 Why have the twins been lucky?
7 Where will Susan sleep?
8 Who will sleep next to her?
9 Why must Susan stop now?
10 Why is Susan thanking her mother?

Vocabulary Definitions

a

The Prince Hamlet is a ...	Die Prinz Hamlet ist eine **Autofähre.**	['ka: 'feri]	**car ferry**
It arrives in Hamburg the ...	Sie kommt am **nächsten Morgen** in Hamburg an.	['nekst 'mɔniŋ]	**next morning**

b

Did you leave your ticket on the table? You're right. I've ... it there.	Hast du deine Fahrkarte auf dem Tisch gelassen? Du hast recht. Ich habe sie dort **gelassen.**	[left]	**left** (to leave)
Have you ... Carol, Eileen?	Hast du Carol **gesehen,** Eileen?	[si:n]	**seen** (to see)
Has she ... tickets for us all?	Hat sie für uns alle Fahrkarten **gekauft?**	[bɔ:t]	**bought** (to buy)
I must tell you about Bill.	Ich muß dir etwas von Bill erzählen.		
No, thanks. Sheila has already ... me.	Nein, danke, Sheila hat es mir schon **erzählt.**	[təuld]	**told** (to tell)
Where's my ...? I must show it when I arrive in England.	Wo ist mein **Reisepaß**? Wenn ich in England ankomme, muß ich ihn vorzeigen.	['pa:spɔ:t]	**passport**
She's ... me this ticket.	Sie hat mir diese Fahrkarte **gegeben.**	[givn]	**given** (to give)
I've just ... from her.	Ich **komme gerade** von ihr.	[kʌm]	**come** (to come)

d

I'm going to eat my roll.	Ich werde mein Brötchen essen.		
Oh, I've already ... my roll.	Ach, ich habe mein Brötchen schon **gegessen.**	['i:tn]	**eaten** (to eat)
I'm going to sleep in my ... now.	Ich werde jetzt in meiner **Kabine** schlafen.	['kæbin]	*cabin*
It is half past eleven now. So I'm very ...	Es ist jetzt halb zwölf. Ich bin also sehr **müde.**	['taiəd]	**tired**
Peggy and Pat Smith are both twelve. They are sisters. They are ...	Peggy und Pat Smith sind beide zwölf. Sie sind Schwestern. Sie sind **Zwillinge.**	[twinz]	**twins**
I want to wash. Have you got a piece of ...?	Ich möchte mich waschen. Hast du ein Stück **Seife**?	[səup]	**soap**
The wind is very fast. There is a ... wind.	Der Wind ist sehr schnell. Es ist ein **starker** Wind.	[strɔŋ]	**strong**
Why is Carol on the floor? She has just ... out of bed.	Warum liegt Carol denn auf dem Fußboden? Sie ist gerade aus dem Bett **gefallen.**	['fɔ:lən]	**fallen** (to fall)
Now the boat is in Hamburg. It has ... Hamburg.	Das Schiff ist nun in Hamburg. Es hat Hamburg **erreicht.**	[ri:tʃt]	**reached** (to reach)
There are lots of men, women and children on deck. There is a big ... there.	Da sind viele Männer, Frauen und Kinder auf dem Deck. Es ist dort eine große **Menschenmenge.**	[kraud]	**crowd**

e

He has had one cup, then another, and now he is drinking his . . . cup.	Er hat eine Tasse getrunken, dann noch eine, und jetzt trinkt er seine **dritte** Tasse.	[θɔːd]	**third**
Carol is the . . . of the school.	Carol ist **Schulsprecherin**.	[ˈhed ˈgəːl]	**head girl**
She is very worried. She is . . .	Sie macht sich viele Gedanken. Sie ist **ängstlich**.	[ˈæŋkʃəs]	*anxious*
She cannot find Pat . . .	Sie kann Pat **nirgendwo** finden.	[ˈæniwɛə]	**anywhere**
Have you searched in all the cabins and in all places? Have you searched . . .?	Hast du in allen Kabinen und an allen Stellen gesucht? Hast du **überall** gesucht?	[ˈevriwɛə]	**everywhere**
She answers = she . . .	sie antwortet = sie **erwidert**.	[riˈplaiz]	**replies** (to reply)
I can't find Pat anywhere. She is . . .	Sie wird **vermißt**.	[ˈmisiŋ]	**missing** (to be missing)
On the deck of the Prince Hamlet there are many . . .	Auf dem Deck der Prinz Hamlet gibt es viele **Rettungsboote**.	[ˈlaifbəut]	**lifeboats**
Has there been an accident? How . . .!	Ist da ein Unfall passiert? Wie **aufregend**!	[ikˈsaitiŋ]	**exciting**
Pat is in one of the boats on deck. She is . . .	Pat ist in einem der Boote auf dem Deck. Sie **sonnt sich**.	[ˈsʌnbeiθiŋ]	**sunbathing** (to sunbathe)
Have you looked everywhere or her? Have you . . . for her?	Hast du nach ihr **gesucht**?	[səːtʃt]	**searched** (to search)

Exercise 2

This . . . is awful.	Diese **Suppe** ist schrecklich.	[suːp]	**soup**
I want to . . . This soup is awful.	Ich möchte mich **beschweren**.	[kəmˈplein]	**complain** (to complain)

Comprehension Exercise 4

That's all, Mum. Thank you for this trip. . . . Susan.	Das ist alles, Mutti. Vielen Dank für diese Fahrt. **Herzliche Grüße**, Susan.	[lʌv]	**love**

Hamburg is famous for its large port.

Unit 11

a

Mr King writes to his wife

1 Dear Joan,
Today my cup **is** dirty.
Yesterday my cup **was** dirty, too.

2 Today I **have** three rolls for breakfast.
Yesterday I **had** only one roll.

3 This morning I **hate** the German tea.
Yesterday I **hated** the German black bread.

4 Today the milk **tastes** awful.
Yesterday the fruit juice **tasted** awful.

5 Today there **are** four old men at my table.
Two days ago there **were** only two old men at my table.

6 I must find a bigger and better hotel.
Hamburg must be nicer than this. I'll write again tomorrow.

Love,
Henry.

Questions

1 How was the cup yesterday?
2 How many rolls did Henry have yesterday?
3 What did he hate yesterday?
4 What was the fruit juice like yesterday?
5 Who was at Henry's table two days ago?

Mrs King's letter

Mrs King writes to Mr King in Hamburg.

Example:
Today I have 3 biscuits for breakfast, yesterday ... (4) ...
Today I have 3 biscuits for breakfast, yesterday **I had 4 biscuits for breakfast.**

Now complete the letter:

Dear Henry,
Today I have 2 rolls for breakfast,
yesterday ... (3)....
Today the milk tastes good,
yesterday ... (awful)....
Today there are four young men at
my table, yesterday ... (2 old men)....
Today the sun is shining,
yesterday ... (sun/not shining)....
Today I have tea for breakfast,
yesterday ... (have coffee)....
Today I hate the cornflakes, yesterday ... (like)....
I hope you'll find a bigger and better hotel.
Love, Joan

b I liked the Rote Grütze

Eileen and Carol are talking about their first lunch in Hamburg.

Eileen: I liked the cold soup for lunch yesterday. What about your lunch?
Carol: Frau Bäcker served Schnitzel. And then we had Rote Grütze. I loved that.
Eileen: I hated the cheese. "Harzer", Christa called it. It tasted like ...
Carol: Don't say it! I had some Harzer an hour ago. It was awful. But the biscuits with white cheese were nice.
Eileen: White cheese? Oh, you mean the Quack?
Carol: Not Quack! Quark, you silly girl.

Questions

1 Did Eileen hate the cold soup?
2 What did Frau Bäcker give Carol for lunch?
3 Did Eileen like the Harzer cheese?
4 When did Carol have some Harzer?
5 What does Eileen call the white cheese?
6 Were the biscuits with white cheese awful?

English food

Carol's German friend Julia tells her about her trip to England and what she thinks of English food.

Example:
Julia: My English family served Irish stew. I loved that.

	...sandwiches	I hated the ...
	...ice-cream	I liked the ...
	...white bread	I loved the ...
	...tea	They were awful.
Go on with:	...coffee	It was awful.
	...orange juice	They were nice.
	...marmalade	It was nice.
	...Irish stew	
	...sausages	

C The city of Hamburg

1 The **city** of Hamburg has a red and white **flag**.

2 Hamburg is **famous** for its Planten un Blomen park and its large **port**.

3 You can't **compare** Hamburg with London. More people live in London than in Hamburg.

4 A lot of people work in the **centre** of Hamburg.

5 The **building opposite** the Alster is the Dresdner Bank.

6 Hamburg is beautiful because there is a lot of **space**.

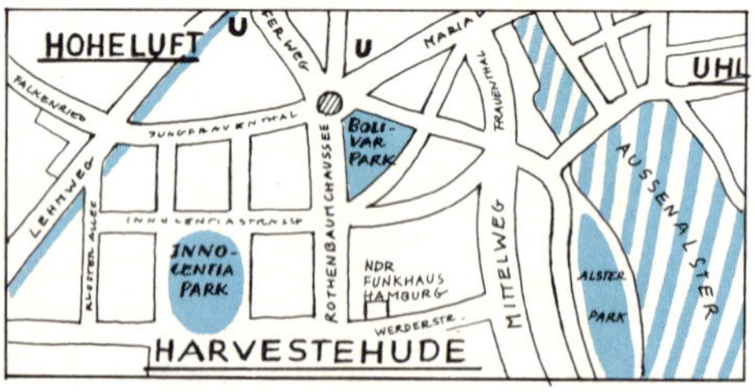

7 Almost every **district** has a park.

8 This is a **stamp** with a picture of a new Hamburg **tube station**.

Questions

1 What sort of flag has the city of Hamburg got?
2 What is Hamburg famous for?
3 Why can't you compare Hamburg and London?
4 Where do a lot of people work?
5 What is the building opposite the Alster?
6 Why is Hamburg so beautiful?
7 Where can you find a park in Hamburg?
8 What is the picture on this stamp?

The City of London

Can you complete this?

The ______________ is very busy.
It is ______________ for
its old buildings like the
Tower and
St. Paul's Cathedral

You can compare London
with Hamburg. London has
many ______________ just like
Hamburg.

A lot of people work in the
______________ of London.
The building opposite the
Houses of Parliament is
Westminster Abbey.

This is a ______________ with a
picture of London. There are a
lot of ______________
in the centre of this city.
This is a ______________

and here is a bus ...
____

Asking the way

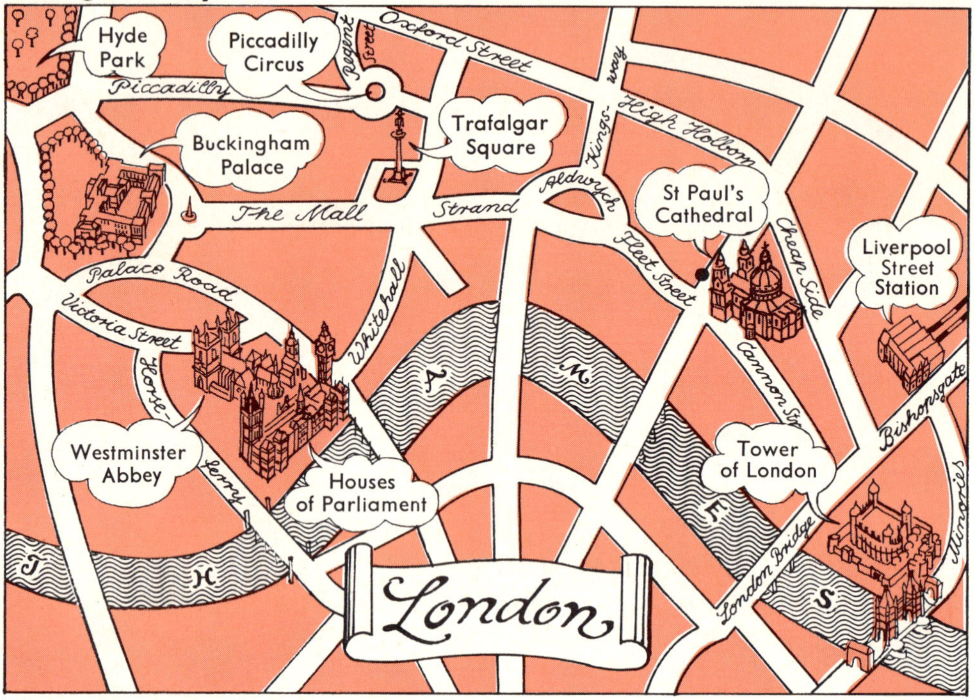

The teacher says: You are standing in front of St Paul's Cathedral. Excuse me, can you tell me the way to the Tower?
Now go on.

d At the Schneiders' flat

1 *Frau Schneider:* Carry David's suitcase into your bedroom, Carsten, and show him where he can put his clothes.

2 *Carsten:* I haven't got much space, I'm afraid, David. You mustn't compare your house with this flat.

3 *David:* It's a very nice flat. And you're lucky to live so near the city centre. What's next to the cinema?

4 *Carsten:* That's a youth hostel. We're in the port district of Hamburg here and we get a lot of tourists and young people.

5 *David:* Is that the Hamburg flag over there?
Carsten: That's right. You can see the old city gate on it.

6 *David:* What are we going to do tomorrow, Carsten?
Carsten: I suggest we cycle to the new Alster tube station. It's very interesting. My uncle works there. He can show us everything.

7 *David:* But I haven't got a bike!
Carsten: You can borrow my father's. He goes to work by bus.

8 *Frau Schneider:* Coffee is ready, children. It's my husband's birthday today, David. So I've baked a big cake.

Questions

1 What does Carsten show David?
2 Why mustn't Carsten compare his house with the flat?
3 Where do the Schneiders live?
4 What is the building next to the cinema?
5 What sort of picture is there on the Hamburg flag?
6 What does Carsten suggest to David?
7 Whose bike can David borrow?
8 Why does Frau Schneider bake a big cake?

e

David's letter

David: I must write home at once. Where can I buy some stamps, please, Carsten?

Carsten: The paper shop opposite sells stamps.
Or you can go to the post office. That's about five minutes from here.
I'll come with you and show you the way.

David: Thanks, I think I still need some help. I don't really know what to say.
How much is a letter to Britain?

Carsten: Seventy Pfennig. How many stamps do you want?

David: Oh, I think a dozen will be enough.

Carsten: Then you just say: Zwölf Marken zu siebzig, bitte.

David: Why 'zu 70'?

Carsten: Well, that means 'stamps at the price of 70 Pfennig'.

David: OK. I understand now.

Questions

1 Which shop sells stamps?
2 How far is it to the post office?
3 How much does a letter from Hamburg to London cost?
4 How many stamps does David want?
5 How do you say in German: a dozen 70 Pfennig stamps?

Partner Work

You are an English tourist. Ask your partner where you can buy stamps, a book about your town, a birthday card, a new suitcase in your town.

You: Excuse me, where can I buy ...?
Partner: Well, the shop in ... strasse sells ...
You: And where is this ... strasse?
Partner: I'll come ...
You: Oh, that's very nice of you. Thank you.

f German food is too good *Listening comprehension dialogue*

Questions

1 Why can't Carol wear her skirt?
   a) she can't wear it because it's new
   b) she can't wear it because it's too old
   c) she can't wear it because she's too fat
   d) she can't wear it because she wants to cycle with it

2 Where does Carol want to go?
   a) to a Hamburg tube station
   b) to a bicycle store
   c) to Herr Bäcker's bike
   d) to a big store

3 Why mustn't Carol eat Torte any more?

a) the skirt will get too big for her
b) ice-cream is better than Torte
c) her old skirt will get too small for her
d) the shop opposite the post office only sells ice-cream

4 What can Carol do for Eileen?

a) She can show Eileen how to make the skirt bigger
b) She can make Eileen's skirt bigger
c) She can make the new skirt bigger
d) She can buy a big ice-cream for her

5 When can Carol buy a big ice-cream for Eileen?

a) After Eileen has made the skirt bigger
b) After Eileen has bought a new skirt
c) After Eileen has cycled to the department store
d) After Eileen has been to the post office

(Text on page 213)

Grammar Practice

1 A Past Tense

"I go to Paris every year."

"I **was** in Paris last year."

I **was** in Hamburg yesterday.
I **had** rolls for breakfast (yesterday).
The coffee **tasted** awful (yesterday).
I **hated** the coffee but I **loved** the rolls (yesterday).
There **were** only five people in the hotel (yesterday).

→ Past Tense of the verb (Simple Past)

1 B

Bei der regelmäßigen Bildung der Zeitform des Past Tense hängen wir **-ed** an:

hate — hated
love — loved
play — played

Diese Form bleibt immer gleich:

I hated the rolls.	We loved the coffee.
He hated the rolls.	They loved the coffee.

} das stumme — "e" fällt debei weg

Diese Formen zu bilden und ihre Besonderheiten zu beachten, dürfte nicht mehr schwierig sein, da wir die -ed Formen des Verbs schon kennen als einen Teil der **Present Perfect** Formen (siehe Unit 4). Nur die besonderen Formen für 'have' und 'be' müssen wir uns hier merken:

I, you, he, she, it, we, they	had	I, he, she, it	was
		you, we, they	were

Das Past Tense bezeichnet ein Geschehen, das in der Vergangenheit abgeschlossen wurde. Wir wenden es also immer an, wenn Wörter im Satz vorkommen wie:

yesterday
last week
last Saturday (Sunday, ...)
last year.

1 C Brian's letter

Brian has his first breakfast with the Schneiders. Frau Schneider serves rolls and black bread. Brian loves the rolls, but he hates the black bread. The milk tastes awful, but the coffee is fine.
Next day Brian is writing a letter about his first breakfast. Now you write this letter for Brian in the past tense.

Dear Mum and Dad,

Yesterday...

Exercises

1 Today everything is OK

Mr King is in a bigger hotel now. At the breakfast table the waiter asks him:
"Do you like our German breakfast?"
Mr King likes it. He tells the waiter everything about the old hotel.

Example:

Mr King: Breakfast is very nice here, but yesterday it was awful.
Waiter: Oh, I'm very glad that you like our hotel.

Go on.

Here	**Yesterday**
have four rolls	one roll
have good coffee	bad coffee
the milk / taste good	awful
be / one young lady at my table	four old men
like the black bread	hate
love the cheese	hate the Harzer
biscuits / be nice	be awful

2 They get up early in Germany

Their German friends want to show the English boys and girls a lot of Germany. So they all have to get up early. Here is Carol's time-table.

a) Now ask questions about what Carol does every day.

Example:
What does Carol do at 6.30?
At 6.30 she gets up.

Look at the list on page 176 and ask your partner.

b) Ask your partner:

When does Carol get up?
When does she . . . ?
. . . ?

3 Happy birthday to you!

It's the same every year with Herrn Schneider's birthday. At 6 o'clock the children **rush** into his bedroom. They **shout**: "Happy birthday to you, Daddy!" Then his wife **serves** him breakfast in bed. He **has** a big piece of cake and two cups of coffee for breakfast. Frau Schneider always **bakes** a nice cake for her husband's birthday. He really **hates** breakfast in bed. He doesn't drink his cup of coffee and his wife **is** angry. He **likes** breakfast in the dining-room better. But he **is** very kind. So he **thanks** them all: "This is very nice of you."
As usual, Frau Schneider's cake **tastes** wonderful. After breakfast he **washes** and **dresses**. He **walks** out of the house and he **suggests** that they all **visit** the famous part of Hamburg or **visit** the cinema. Carsten **compares** the two suggestions and **decides** that the cinema opposite the old city gate **has** the best film in town. After work Mr Schneider **looks** at all his presents and **thanks** his wife and his children. Then they **walk** to the cinema. They all **like** the film, **it's** an interesting Western.

a) David wants to know:

What happened on your father's birthday last year, Carsten?
You are Carsten. Be careful with "we, they, I, he" etc.

Begin like this:

Last year my father's birthday was the same as today. At 6 o'clock we rushed into . . .

b) David writes a letter to his parents. He liked the story about Herr Schneider's birthday.

Dear Mother and Father,

Today it was Herrn Schneider's 44th birthday. At 6 o'clock in the morning, the children . . .

Love,

David

12 HDYD CS 2 Textbook 42920

4 Katja's holiday in England

In England the boys and girls didn't get up as early as in Germany. Katja was in England last year. Here is her time-table.

Time-table in England

7.30 get up
8.15 have an English breakfast
8.30 read the newspaper
8.45 walk to school
12.20 have dinner at school
16.00 walk home to the English family

19.30 visit the Bingo Hall (Monday)
listen to Carol's records of the Beatles (Tuesday)
watch TV (Wednesday)
visit a pop concert (Wednesday)
bake an English cake (Thursday)
walk to Piccadilly (Friday)
visit the Tower (Saturday)
wait for telephone call from Mummy (Sunday)

Look at Katja's time-table and write what she did last year.

Example:

She got up at 7.45. At a quarter to nine she walked to school ...

5 Carol's letter

Carol writes a letter to her parents in England. She writes what they did on Saturday. Look at Exercise 2 and write the letter.

6 Where is my shopping-bag?

Find the past tense form of these verbs and fill in the blanks: show, walk, have, be, like, order, taste, serve, like, offer, arrive, look, hate, wait, ask, remember

Yesterday I looked into some Hamburg shops. I ... the big department stores. Two hours later with two bags full of things we ... very hungry. In the cafeteria of a big shop they ... Wiener Schnitzel. It was the meal of the day for only six Marks.

We ... to wait for ten minutes, then the waiter ... He ... Spanish and didn't speak German well and he didn't understand English. We ... two Schnitzels and then we ... for 25 minutes. Then he ... us something called "Rote Grütze". It ... awful and I ... it. But Brian ... it very much.
When we ... the waiter for our Schnitzel he ... very sorry. He ... to take the Rote Grütze away and bring us the Schnitzels instead. But we ... hungry and ... out. Five minutes later I ... my shopping-bags. They ... to be in the cafeteria, still. We ... back to the cafeteria quickly, but the two bags ... not there any more. The waiter... at us, laughed and ... us the bags on a chair. This was our lucky day.

Vocabulary Definitions

a

Please wash that cup. It is very ...	Sie ist sehr **schmutzig**.	['dəːti]	**dirty**
Today is Tuesday, and ... was Monday.	Und **gestern** war Montag.	['jestədei]	**yesterday**
Today I am happy. And yesterday I ... happy, too.	Heute bin ich glücklich. Und gestern **war** ich auch glücklich.	[wəz]	**was** (to be)
Today I hate milk in tea. And yesterday I ... it too.	Heute mag ich **keine** Milch im Tee. Und gestern **mochte** ich es auch **nicht**.	[heitid]	**hated** (to hate)
Today the coffee tastes awful. And yesterday it ... awful, too.	Heute schmeckt der Kaffee furchtbar. Und gestern **schmeckte** er auch furchtbar.	[teistid]	**tasted** (to taste)
Today there are 31 pupils in my class. And yesterday there ... 31, too.	Heute sind 31 Schüler in meiner Klasse. Und gestern **waren** es auch 31.	[wəː]	**were** (to be)

b

It is an awful cheese. The Germans ... it 'Harzer'.	Das ist ein furchtbarer Käse. Die Deutschen **nennen** ihn ‚Harzer'.	[kɔːl]	**call** (to call)
I had some Harzer 60 minutes ago. I had it an ... ago.	Ich aß etwas Harzerkäse vor einer **Stunde**.	['auə]	**hour**

c

Hamburg is a big town. It is a ...	Hamburg ist eine große Stadt. Es ist eine **Großstadt**.	['siti]	**city**
Hamburg's ... is red and white.	Hamburgs **Flagge** ist rotweiß.	[flæg]	**flag**
Hamburg is ... for its beautiful parks.	Hamburg ist **berühmt** für seine schönen Parks.	['feiməs]	**famous**
Hamburg, Rotterdam and London are large ...	Hamburg, Rotterdam und London sind große **Häfen**.	[pɔːts]	**ports**

London is bigger than Hamburg. You cannot . . . Hamburg and London.	London ist größer als Hamburg. Man kann Hamburg und London nicht **vergleichen.**	[kəm'pɛə]	**compare** (to compare)
The Alster is in the middle of Hamburg. It is in the . . . of Hamburg.	Die Alster ist mitten in Hamburg. Sie ist im **Zentrum** von Hamburg.	['sentə]	*centre*
A house or a bank or a station is a . . .	Ein Haus, eine Bank oder ein Bahnhof sind **Gebäude.**	[bildiŋ]	**building**
The bank is not on this side of the Alster. It is on the . . . side.	Die Bank ist nicht auf dieser Seite der Alster. Sie ist **auf der anderen Seite.**	['ɔpəzit]	**opposite**
You have too much furniture in this room. There is not enough . . .	Sie haben zu viele Möbel in diesem Raum. Da ist nicht genügend **Platz.**	[speis]	**space**
St. Pauli and Eppendorf are . . . of Hamburg.	St. Pauli und Eppendorf sind **Stadtteile** von Hamburg.	['distrikts]	*districts*
I want to send a letter to Sheila. Have you got a . . .?	Ich möchte Sheila einen Brief schicken. Hast du mal eine **Briefmarke?**	[stæmp]	**stamp**
On the stamp is a picture of a new Hamburg . . . station.	Auf der Briefmarke ist ein Bild von einem neuen Hamburger **Untergrundbahnhof.**	[tju:b]	**tube**

d

A house has four or five rooms. A . . . often has only 2 or 3 rooms.	Ein Haus hat vier oder fünf Zimmer. Eine **Wohnung** hat oftmals nur 2 oder 3 Zimmer.	[flæt]	**flat**
You can put your blazer and your other . . . in the cupboard.	Du kannst deinen Blazer und deine andere **Kleidung** in den Schrank tun.	[kləuðz]	**clothes**
Let's go and see the Sophia Loren film at the . . .	Laß uns den Film mit Sophia Loren im **Kino** sehen.	['sinəmə]	**cinema**
On the Hamburg flag you can see the old city . . .	Auf der Hamburger Flagge kann man das alte **Stadttor** sehen.	[geit]	**gate**
I've got a good idea: Let's cycle to the Alster. I . . . we cycle.	Ich habe eine gute Idee: Laßt uns mit dem Rad an die Alster fahren. Ich **schlage vor,** wir fahren mit dem Rad.	[sə'dʒest]	**suggest** (to suggest)
Can you lend me your bike, please? Yes, OK, you can . . . it.	Kannst du mir bitte dein Rad leihen? Ja, sicher kannst du es dir **leihen.** (lend — jemandem etwas leihen; borrow — **sich** etwas leihen)	['bɔrəu]	**borrow** (to borrow)
Your father's brother is your . . .	Der Bruder deines Vaters ist dein **Onkel.**	[ʌnkl]	*uncle*
I'm 12 years old today. It's my . . .	Heute bin ich zwölf Jahre alt. Ich habe **Geburtstag.**	['bə:θdei]	**birthday**
I've . . . a cake for your birthday party.	Ich habe einen Kuchen **gebacken** für deine Geburtstagsparty.	[beikt]	*baked* (to bake)

e

I want 12 stamps. I want a . . .	Ich möchte gern 12 Briefmarken. Ich möchte ein **Dutzend.**	[dʌzn]	**dozen**
"12 zu siebzig" means "12 stamps at the . . . of 70 Pf."	"12 zu siebzig" 12 "Briefmarken zu einem **Preis** von 70 Pf."	[prais]	**price**

Unit 12

a David at a Hamburg school

Frau Schneider: Did you take David to all your lessons, Carsten?
Carsten: Yes, I did.
Frau Schneider: And did you introduce him to your headmaster?
Carsten: No, I didn't. The headmaster wasn't in his office. But I showed David the whole school and I introduced him to our English teacher.
Frau Schneider: What did he ask you, David?
David: Oh, he asked me about my school in Worcester.
Carsten: Yes, and then David talked for ten minutes about his school in front of the whole class. It was great!

Questions

Answer with "Yes, he did" or "No, he didn't".

1 Did Carsten invite David to all his lessons?
2 Did Carsten introduce David to his headmaster?
3 Did he show David the whole school?
4 Did he introduce him to his English teacher?
5 Did the English teacher ask David about his school?
6 Did David sing English songs in front of the whole class?
7 Did he talk about English meals?
8 Did he talk for ten minutes about his school?

b In the High Street

This is a **music** shop. **Next-door** is a shop with **glasses** in the window. A lady is **crossing** the street to the **glove** shop.

Now the lady is buying a **handbag**. The assistant is giving her a **bill**. The lady has got her **purse** in her hand. She is handing the manager a ten-pound note.

Questions

1 Is this a grocer's shop?
2 What is in the window of the shop next-door?
3 What is the lady doing?
4 What is the lady buying?
5 What is the assistant doing now?
6 What has the lady got in her hand?

At the shops

Can you complete this? Look at page 182 again.

This is the High Street. There are a lot of shops in this street. The biggest shop is a ... ... there is a shop with ... in the window. The lady is ... the street to the ...
Now we are in one of these shops. A lady is buying a ... The assistant is giving her a ... The lady has got her ... in her hand.

C An unlucky afternoon

Three days before his journey back to Worcester, David cycled to a big Hamburg department store. Carsten did not want to go with him. He had too much homework. So David had to choose the presents for his parents without him. He wanted something really nice for his mother — a silver spoon of Hamburg or a pair of gloves or perhaps a handbag.
Everybody in the department store was very helpful. The assistant in the glove department showed him a lovely black handbag. But he did not have enough money. So he had to buy some gloves instead of the bag.
Then he crossed the road to another shop. There were some very nice German beer-glasses there — just the right present for his father.
"16,50 DM", said the assistant to him. David handed her a twenty-mark note and then rushed to the music shop next-door. He wanted to buy a German record for his sister. But there were so many, it was not easy to choose.

David was very thirsty now and crossed the road again — he wanted to go into the cafeteria of the department store. There he ordered a coca-cola. He quickly finished the glass and wanted to pay. But his purse was not in his pocket!
"I'm afraid my purse has disappeared," he said to the assistant behind the counter.
"Don't make me laugh!" said the assistant, and called the manager.
"Ah, another little thief," said the manager to David. "Let's see what you've got in the parcel. Gloves, eh? Did you pay for them?"
"Of course I did."
"Where's the bill then?"
"In my purse," said David, "and my purse . . ."
"Yes, I know your story. You haven't got your purse."
At that moment the girl from the record shop appeared in the cafeteria.
"Ah, there you are," she said to David. "You are a silly boy! Why did you leave your purse on our counter?"
"Thank you, thank you very much, Fräulein," said David. "You're wonderful!"

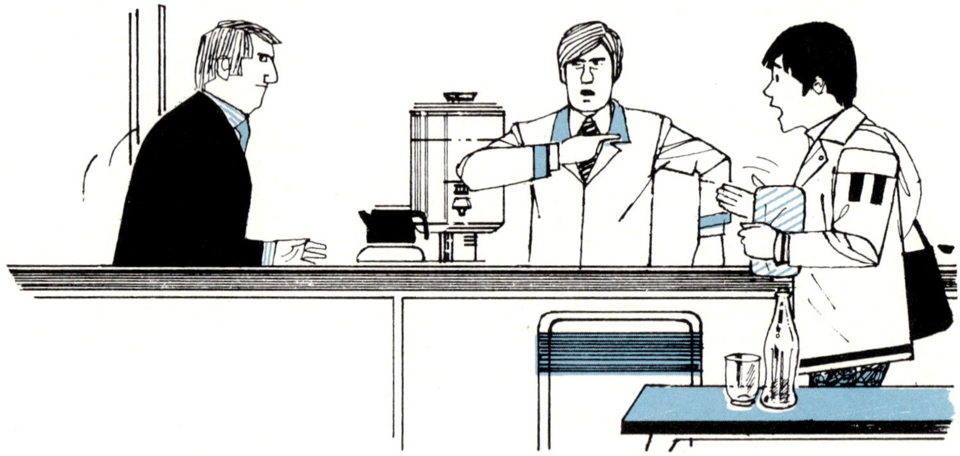

Can you find the right answer?

1 Where did David cycle three days before his journey back to Worcester?

a) to the Reeperbahn.
b) to a big Hamburg restaurant.
c) to a small Hamburg department store
d) to a big Hamburg department store

2 Who did not want to go with him?

a) Susan didn't
b) the assistant didn't
c) Carsten didn't
d) Bernd didn't

3 What did David want to buy for his mother?

a) a pair of gloves, a handbag or a silver spoon
b) a handbag or a silver spoon or a pair of gloves
c) a silver spoon and a handbag and a pair of gloves
d) a silver spoon and a handbag or a pair of gloves

4 What did he buy in the department store?

a) a bag and some gloves
b) a bag instead of some gloves
c) a pair of gloves
d) a handbag

5 What did David buy for his father and sister?

a) a beer-glass for his sister and a record for his father
b) a record for his father and his sister
c) a record player for his sister and a beer-glass for his father
d) a beer-glass for his father and a German record for his sister

6 Why did David cross the road again?

a) because he wanted to pay for all the presents
b) because he wanted to go to the department store to buy some presents
c) because he was thirsty and wanted to drink a coke
d) because his purse was not in his pocket

7 Why did the assistant call the manager?

a) because David had a parcel in his hands
b) because David's purse was not in his pocket
c) because David was a thief
d) because she wanted to see what there was in David's parcel

Questions

1 Why didn't Carsten want to come with David?
2 Why did David want to cycle to the department store?
3 What did the assistant show him first?
4 What did David have to buy instead?
5 What did David want to buy for his father?
6 What did David order in the cafeteria?
7 Why didn't David pay at once?
8 What did the assistant do?
9 What did the manager say to David?
10 Where had David's purse been all the time?

d

The weather map

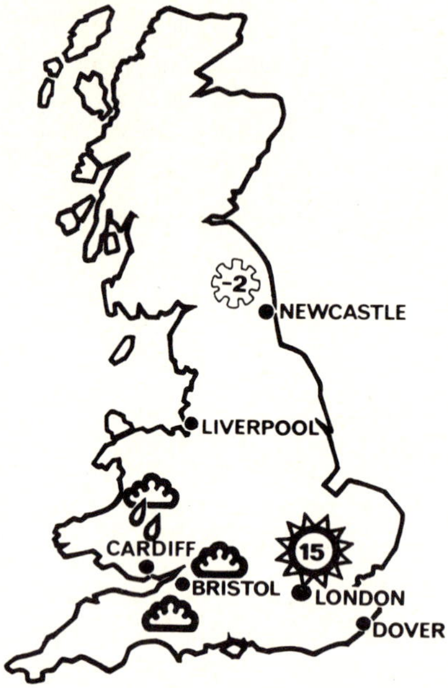

It will be cold in Newcastle
but **warm** and **sunny** in London.
There will be rain in Cardiff
and it will be **cloudy** in Bristol.

Tomorrow's weather

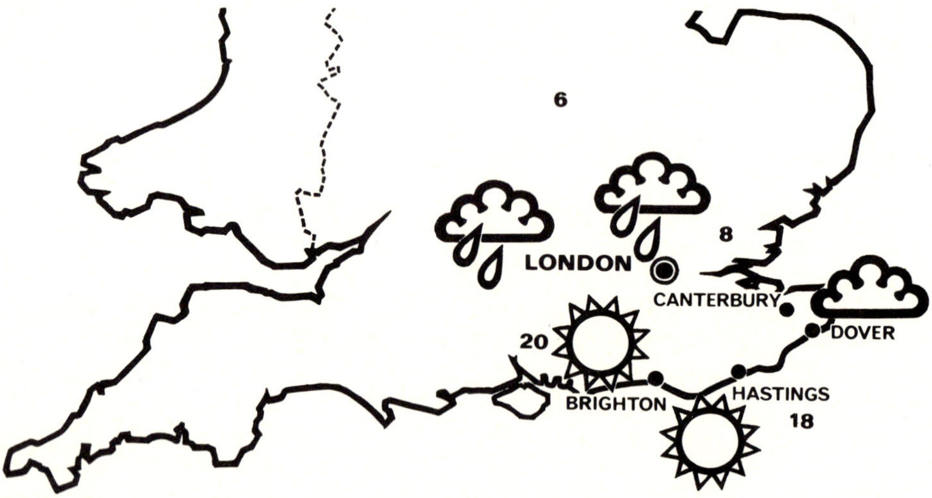

Can you complete this weather forecast?

It will be . . . and . . . in Brighton. There will be . . . in London and it will be . . .
It will be . . . in Dover. It will be . . . and . . . in Hastings.

e The weather forecast

David: Did you hear the weather forecast this morning, Carsten?
Carsten: No, I didn't, but perhaps my mother did.
What did they say, Mum? Will it be fine today?
Frau Schneider: No, I'm afraid it won't. There will be some rain later this morning, and it'll be cloudy this afternoon. Why don't you make your trip tomorrow? It'll be warm and sunny then.
Carsten: Don't worry, Mum. The forecast is often wrong.
We'll just go out to Hagenbeck and hope for the best.

Questions

1 Did Carsten hear the weather forecast?
2 What will the weather be like this morning?
3 What will the weather be like this afternoon?
4 What will the weather be like tomorrow?
5 Why mustn't Carsten's mother worry?

Partner work

Now work with your partner and ask him about the weather:

You: Did you listen to the weather forecast this morning?
Did you see the weather map on TV / in the paper?
What did they say on the radio about the weather?
Will it be fine? / Warm or cold? / Sunny or cloudy?
What about the forecast for tomorrow / the rest of the week?
What is the forecast for Berlin / Hamburg / Stuttgart / Bonn?

Partner: I'm afraid I did not see the weather map on TV.
I did not hear the forecast on the radio, but I'm hoping for the best / my mother says it'll be ...
The forecast is so often wrong, why do you worry about the weather?
It'll be warmer/colder in Berlin than in Stuttgart/Bonn/Hamburg.

f This is what you say in English

You want to find out what people think. So you say:

Did you like the dialogue/story/text/picture/film?
Didn't the boy/star/woman look nice/awful/pretty?
What did you think of the ending/the beginning/the middle?
Did you think the exercises were too difficult/too easy?
What was your opinion of the tape/the music/the lesson?
Did you understand everything?
Did you make any mistakes?
What about the lesson today? Was it interesting/boring/exciting/good?

Now ask your partner about the story in Unit 10 (A girl in the water), the dialogue in Unit 11 (At the Schneiders' flat), the pictures in Unit 9, the lesson last Thursday.

Grammar Practice

1 A Did you . . .?

"**Did** you **buy** that cheese **last year**?"
"No, I **didn't.** It was yesterday."

1 B

Present Tense

(always, often)
? → do, does
no, not→ don't, doesn't

Past Tense

(yesterday, last year)
? → did
no, not→ didn't

Wir wissen, daß im Present Tense bei Fragen und bei Sätzen mit 'no' oder 'not' das Hilfsverb 'do' oder 'does' eingesetzt wird. Das Hauptverb erscheint dann in der Grundform (Infinitiv): **Do** you always **cycle** to school? Yes, I **do.**

Im Past Tense verwenden wir entsprechend die Vergangenheitsform 'did': **Did** you **buy** that cheese last year? No, I **didn't.**
Das gleiche gilt für die Kurzformen:

Yes, I do	Yes, I did.
No, I don't.	No, I didn't.

1 C

	Brian		cycle to school.
Does	Tina		sing English songs.
	your friend	always	buy things in a department store.
	Brian and Tina	often	go into a cafeteria.
Do	you	usually	buy pop records.
	your friends		go swimming.

	Brian	cycle to school	
	Tina	sing English songs	yesterday.
	your friend	buy things in a department store	last week.
Did	Brian and Tina	go into a cafeteria	last year.
	you	buy pop records	
	your friends	go swimming	

Now write some of these questions and answer them.

1 Does your friend often buy pop records? Yes, he does.
2 Did you go into a cafeteria yesterday? No, I didn't.
3 Do . . .
4 . . .
5 . . .
6 . . .

Exercises

1 What did you do yesterday?

Answer the following questions with "Yes, I did" or "No, I didn't."

1 Did you cycle to school in the morning?
2 Did you buy a record for your sister yesterday?
3 Did you watch TV last night?
4 Did you drink coke for lunch?
5 Did you go to a big department store after school?
6 Did you write a letter in your English lesson?
7 Did you learn a song at school?
8 Did you do your homework in the afternoon?

2 The weather forecast

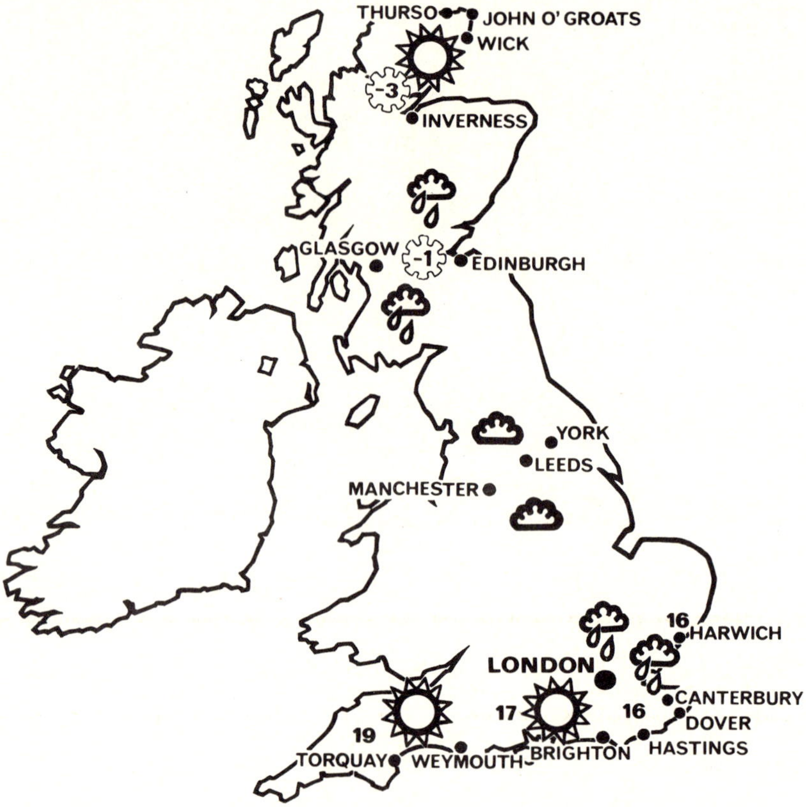

a) Now you are the television announcer. Start your weather report like this:

This is the BBC with tomorrow's weather.
It will be ... in and in ...
There will be ... in and in ...
It will be ...

End like this:

So it will be a fine day in the south. Don't forget your umbrellas in the north. Bye-bye for today. This was your friendly BBC weather service. Good night. Sleep well.

b) Compare the temperatures. Use the words "warm, hot, cold".

Example:
In London it will be colder than in Brighton.

Now go on.

3 David's diary — Davids Tagebuch

David writes down what he does every day. Here is a page of his diary.

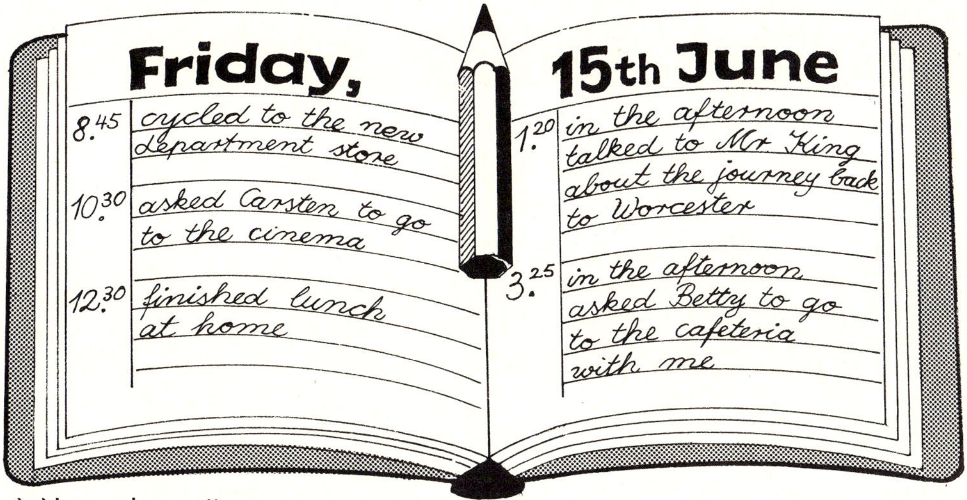

a) Now ask questions.

Example:
What did David do at ... o'clock?
At ... o'clock he ...

b) Ask more questions.

Example:
When did David go to the new department store?
He cycled there at a quarter to eight.

4 Did you like the journey to England last summer?

Ask your neighbour:

Did you buy a	present		mother
	pair of gloves		brother
	pair of glasses		father
	purse	for your	sister
	handbag		grandfather
	beer-glass		grandmother
	silver spoon		uncle
	record		aunt

Answer with:

Yes, I did, but it wasn't easy to choose.
No, I didn't, but I bought a ... instead of the ...

5 What did you do at school today?

Your mother asks a lot of questions like these:

Did you like school today?
Did you learn any new English words?
Did your teacher give you a lot of homework?
Did you get back your Maths test?
Did your teacher ask you anything in German?

Your mother wants to know everything.
Find her questions. This list can help you:

Example:

(you / like) school
Did you like school?

(you / listen) to the teacher
(you / see) Tom Brown in school today
(your German teacher / give you) your German test
(your English teacher / look at) yesterday's homework
(you / make a lot of noise) in the lessons

Did you cycle to school today?

Vocabulary Definitions

a

... take Brian to all your lessons yesterday? Yes, ...	**Hast du** Brian gestern in alle deine Stunden mitgenommen? Ja.	['didjə]	**did you**
(**'I did'** kann man nicht übersetzen, im Deutschen wiederholen wir das Verb nur, wenn wir etwas ganz besonders betonen.)		[ai'did]	**I did**
The headmaster wasn't in his ...	Der Schulleiter war nicht in seinem **Büro**.	['ɔfis]	**office**
I showed Brian all the classrooms. I showed him the ... school.	Ich zeigte Brian alle Klassenzimmer. Ich zeigte ihm die **ganze** Schule.	[həul]	**whole**

b

Where can I buy a record here? Go to a ... shop.	Wo kann ich hier eine Schallplatte kaufen? Geh in ein **Musik**geschäft.	['mju:sik]	*music*
Beside that shop is another shop. ... is another shop.	Neben dem Geschäft ist ein weiteres Geschäft. **Direkt daneben** ist ein anderes Geschäft.	['nekst'dɔ:]	**next-door**
Ah, there's Bob. Have some beer, Bob. Get a ... for Bob's beer, Fred.	Ach, da ist ja Bob. Trink ein Bier mit, Bob. Fred, hol mal ein **Glas** für Bobs Bier.	[gla:s]	*glass*
You must go across that street. ... that street.	Sie müssen über die Straße dort gehen. Sie müssen die Straße dort **überqueren**.	[krɔs]	**cross** (to cross)
My hands are cold. Then why don't your wear ...?	Meine Hände sind kalt. Warum trägst du denn keine **Handschuhe**?	[glʌvz]	**gloves**
Where's your purse, Mary? It's in my ...	Wo ist deine Geldbörse, Mary? Sie ist in meiner **Handtasche**.	['hændbæg]	**handbag**
Waiter, I want to pay, please. Can I have my ...?	Ober, ich möchte bitte zahlen. Kann ich die **Rechnung** bekommen?	[bil]	**bill**

c

Before his trip back to England. Three days before his ...	Vor seiner Fahrt zurück nach England. Drei Tage vor seiner **Reise**.	['dʒə:ni]	**journey**
I want to choose a nice ... for his birthday.	Ich möchte ein nettes **Geschenk** zu seinem Geburtstag aussuchen.	['presənt]	**present**
Is Mary coming with you? No, I'm going ... her.	Kommt Mary mit dir? Nein, ich gehe **ohne** sie.	[wið'aut]	**without**
Do you want sugar in your tea? You do? Then take this ...	Möchtest du Zucker im Tee? Ja? Dann nimm diesen **Silberlöffel**.	['silvə 'spu:n]	*silver spoon*
I do not want one glove. I want a ... of gloves.	Ich möchte nicht einen Handschuh. Ich möchte ein **Paar** Handschuhe.	[pɛə]	**pair**
All the pupils in my class must come. ... must come.	Alle Schüler meiner Klasse müssen kommen. **Jeder** muß kommen.	['evribɔdi]	**everybody**
Everybody wanted to help. They were all ...	Sie waren alle **hilfreich**.	['helpful]	**helpful**
He did not find a nice bag. He had to buy some gloves ... the bag.	Er fand keine nette Tasche. Er mußte Handschuhe **anstelle** der Tasche kaufen.	[in'sted əv]	**instead of**
The opposite of 'difficult' is ...	Das Gegenteil von 'schwierig' ist **'leicht'**.	['i:si]	**easy**
It is very hot. So I am very ... and must have a coca-cola.	Also bin ich sehr **durstig**.	['θə:sti]	**thirsty**

13 HDYD CS 2 Textbook 42920

The boy's purse was not in his . . .	Die Geldbörse des Jungen war nicht in seiner **Tasche**.	[ˈpɔkit]	**pocket**
	(bag = Tasche, die man mit sich trägt; pocket = Mantel-, Hosen- oder Jackentasche)		
Why did you leave your purse on the . . . in my shop?	Warum hast du dein Portemonnaie auf dem **Ladentisch** gelassen?	[ˈkauntə]	**counter**

d

The . . . will be warm and sunny tomorrow.	Das **Wetter** wird morgen warm und sonnig sein.	[ˈweðə]	**weather**
The opposite of 'cold' is . . .	Das Gegenteil von ‚kalt' ist **‚warm'**.	[wɔːm]	*warm*
You are nice and brown, Fred.	Du bist schön braun, Fred.		
Yes, it was nice and . . . in Benidorm.	Ja, es war schön und **sonnig** in Benidorm.	[ˈsʌni]	**sunny**
It will not be sunny in Bristol but . . .	In Bristol wird es nicht sonnig sein, sondern **wolkig/bedeckt**.	[ˈklaudi]	**cloudy**

e

Will it be warm and sunny tomorrow? I don't know. Get your radio and listen to the . . .	Wird es morgen warm und sonnig sein? Das weiß ich nicht. Hol dein Radio und höre die **Wettervorhersage**.	[ˈweðə ˈfɔːkaːst]	**weather forecast**

f

You want to . . . what people think.	Du möchtest **herausfinden**, was die Leute denken.	[faind ˈaut]	**find out** (to find out)
What do you think of the story?	Wie denkst du über die Geschichte?		
What is your . . . of the story?	Was ist deine **Meinung** von der Geschichte?	[əˈpinjən]	**opinion**
The . . . is the opposite of the beginning.	‚Der **Schluß**' ist das Gegenteil von ‚der Anfang'.	[ˈendiŋ]	**ending**
Have you got this music on . . .?	Hast du diese Musik auf **Band**?	[teip]	**tape**
The opposite of 'exciting' is . . .	Das Gegenteil von ‚aufregend' ist **‚langweilig'**.	[ˈbɔːriŋ]	**boring**

The forecast is often wrong. We'll go to out to Hagenbeck.

Unit 13

a The thief in the cinema

1 Last Thursday, David **went** with Eileen to a Hamburg cinema.

2 They **sat** at the front because the seats **were** cheaper there.

3 David **bought** two ice-creams for them,

4 and they **ate** them during the film.

5 Then a young man **came** in and **sat** down beside Eileen.

6 Two minutes later, the man **got** up again and **left** the cinema with a girl.

7 David **saw** he had a large rucksack.

8 Ten minutes later, Eileen shouted, "That man **took** my handbag! Come on, David, quick! We must follow him."

Questions

1 Where did David go with Eileen?
2 Where did they sit?
3 What did David buy?
4 When did they eat them?
5 Where did the young man sit down?
6 When did the young man get up again?
7 What did David see?
8 What did the young man take?

He didn't like that film!

Example:

Every Thursday Tom **goes** to the cinema.	Last Thursday he **went** to the cinema, too.

Now it's your turn:

Usually he **sits** in a cheap seat,	but last Thursday he ... in an expensive seat
Usually he **buys** one ice-cream,	but last Thursday he ... two ice-creams.
Every Thursday he **comes** in at 8 o'clock,	but last Thursday he ... in at a quarter past 8.
Every Thursday he **sits** down at once,	but last Thursday he ... down after Eileen.
Usually he **eats** the ice-cream alone,	but last week he ... it with Eileen.
Usually he **gets** up and **leaves** the cinema after the film,	but last Thursday Eileen didn't like the film and so they ... and ... the cinema before the film was over.
	He'll never invite a girl to a film again.

b At a Hamburg police station

1 *Policeman:* And when did you leave the cinema?
David: Oh, we left it half an hour ago.

2 *David:* We tried to follow the man with the rucksack, but we couldn't find him in Mönkebergstraße.

3 *Policeman:* Where did you sit in the cinema? At the back?
Eileen: No, we sat in the cheaper seats at the front.

4 *Policeman:* Could you see what the man had on?
David: I only saw his dirty white trousers. Ah, yes — he had very long black hair.

5 *Policeman:* Well, that's useful. Did he leave the cinema alone?
David: No, he didn't. He left it with a girl.

6 *Policeman:* Then I think I know who he is. He came to Hamburg three months ago with his wife Roberta.

7 *Policeman:* We call him Heini von Langfinger. He always works in cinemas; but I know where we can find him.

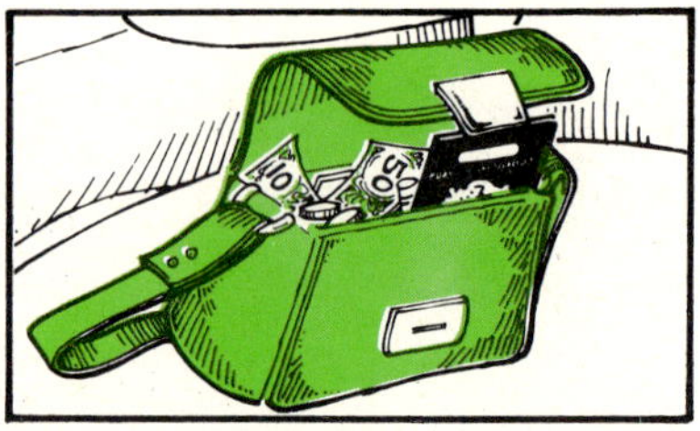

8 *Policeman:* Did you have your passport in your handbag, Miss?

Eileen: Yes, I did. Isn't it awful? What can I do now?

9 *Policeman:* Don't worry. We'll get your handbag back for you. Just give me your telephone number and ...

10 *Speaker:* Well, Eileen was lucky. The police found Heini in the Café Keese with the handbag and the passport and Eileen's money.

Questions

1 When did David and Eileen leave the cinema?
2 What did they try to do?
What couldn't they do?
4 What did the young man wear?
What sort of hair had he got?
5 With whom did the young man leave the cinema?
6 When did Heini come to Hamburg?
What was his wife's name?
8 What did Eileen have in her handbag?
10 Where did the police find Heini?

A policeman's questions

Susan and Inge went to a Hamburg police station. A policeman asked them a lot of questions about the thief and the purse.

Now you act the scene:

Policeman: Good morning. Can I help you?
Susan: Yes, a thief took my purse at the new cafeteria.

Go on and ask the policeman's questions:

Example:

Policeman:	*Susan:*
leave the cafeteria (when)	half past three
When did you leave the cafeteria?	I left at half past three.

sit (where)	next to the counter
the man / wear (what)	blue jeans
he / leave the cafeteria (when)	at twenty past three
he / leave the cafeteria without his girl friend	Yes/No
you / have a lot of money in the purse	Yes/No
you / have your passport in the purse, too	Yes

Susan: Isn't it awful? What can I do now?
Policeman: Don't worry, we know that man. We call him Heini von Langfinger.

C

Can I borrow your camera?

Gisela: I'm going down to the port tomorrow. Can I borrow your camera, Dad?

Father: You know I don't lend my camera to **anybody**, Gisela.

Gisela: **May** I **use** your cassette recorder, then?

Father: No, you may not. I'm sorry, Gisela, but I must **refuse**. You took my cassette recorder last week and then left it in the cinema. But I'll tell you what I'll do: I'll come with you and we can take some pictures **together**. What do you think of that idea?

Gisela: Great!

Questions

1 What does Gisela want to borrow?
2 Why doesn't she get it from her father?
3 What does she want to borrow after that?
4 Why does her father refuse again?
5 What does her father suggest instead?
6 Does Gisela like the idea?

Where are you going tomorrow?

Talk to your partner.

to the seaside / downtown / shopping / to a party

I'm going ... tomorrow.
Can I borrow your ...

car / camera / record-player / bike

You know I don't lend my ...
to anybody, Pam.

May I use your ... then?

No, you may not. I'm sorry,
Pam, but I must refuse.

d Eileen's school photographs

1 I took this photograph at our school dance. David **made a speech**.

2 This is our class. We **stood** in front of the school for this photograph.

3 This is Ken. He stood behind me. He's the tallest boy in the school, and the most **handsome**.

4 This is Bill. He is an **interpreter** now and **translates** German letters into English.

5 **Sometimes** Bill welcomes guests from **foreign** countries — from France or Spain or Holland.

6 He can speak four **languages**.

7 Behind Bill you will **notice** Gwen. She's the **cleverest** girl in the photograph. She's a professor now.

Questions

1 What did David do?
2 Where did they stand?
3 Does Ken look awful?
4 What does Bill do?
5 Who does Bill sometimes welcome?
6 How many languages can he speak?
7 Is Gwen a silly girl?

David's friends

Can you complete this?

I . . . this photograph at the seaside. We were standing in front of the cafeteria. This is Sally. She is the . . . girl. Tom . . . . . . Carsten. Bob is the most . . . boy. This is Julia. She . . . German letters into English. She is an . . . now. Sometimes she goes to . . . countries — to France, Spain or Holland. She can speak five . . . In front of Julia you will . . . Katja. She is the . . . girl in the photograph.

Use these words or a form of these words:

handsome languages interpreter clever notice stand tall translate take foreign near

Compare these boys and girls

Look at these boys and girls and compare them:

Example:

Julia's hair is **longer than** Tom's.
Sally is not **as tall as** Bob. Tom is **the tallest** boy in the photo.

Go on now. Compare their hair, shirts, trousers, shoes and skirts.

e The dance

On the last day of David's holiday in Hamburg, Carsten took him to the international party at his school. All the Worcester boys and girls and their Hamburg partners were there.
The party began at seven o'clock. The headmaster welcomed the guests. Then he made a speech about international friendship. Carol's friend Gisela was the interpreter. She translated everything into English. Then everybody danced. There was a disco with plenty of good records. It was great.
Then Gisela noticed Belinda. Belinda did not dance. She stood alone in a corner. Gisela could not understand that. Belinda had the most beautiful eyes and the longest legs of all the Worcester girls. Why didn't the Hamburg boys dance with her?
At that moment Gerd Kaiser sat down beside Belinda. Gerd was the tallest and most handsome boy at the Hamburg school. He was clever, too, and good at Maths — but he did not know much English. And Belinda's German was even worse than his English.
So Gisela went and sat down beside them and translated for them. Five minutes later, Gerd asked Belinda for the next dance. They danced all evening and seemed very happy.
And Gisela thought, "A foreign language can really be very useful."

Find the right answers

1 When did Carsten take David to the party?

a) on the last day of June
b) last Saturday
c) the day before David left Hamburg
d) on the last day of Carsten's holiday

2 When did the party begin?

a) at seven o'clock in the morning
b) after lunch
c) in the evening
d) in the afternoon

3 Who was the interpreter?

a) Carol
b) Gisela's friend
c) the headmaster
d) a German girl

4 What did the interpreter do?

a) she translated a letter into English
b) she translated everything into French
c) she didn't translate everything into English
d) she translated the speech into English

5 Who did Gisela notice?

a) Betty
b) Carsten
c) Belinda
d) Carol

6 Why did she notice her?

a) she danced well
b) she didn't dance
c) she stood in the corner with some friends
d) she didn't want to dance

7 Why didn't the Hamburg boys dance with Belinda?

a) because she had the most beautiful eyes
b) because Gisela couldn't understand that
c) because Belinda couldn't understand German
d) because Gerd Kaiser couldn't understand German

8 What did Gisela think?

a) the English language can be really useful
b) the German language can be really useful
c) all languages like French and Spanish can be useful
d) only the English language can be useful

Questions

1 Where did Carsten take David on the last day?
2 When did the party begin?
3 What did the headmaster do at the party?
4 What did Gisela do at the party?
5 Could Gisela understand Belinda?
6 Who was Gerd?
7 How much English did Gerd know?
8 Was Belinda's German better?
9 What did Gerd do then?
10 What did Gisela think?

Grammar Practice

1 A He **went** down to the river . . .

'It was in 1912, on a fine morning in June.
I **went** down to the river . . .

1 B Past Tense of Irregular verbs

She **saw** a film in the cinema
and **came** home late.
She **sat** down in the kitchen
and **ate** some cornflakes.

In Unit 10 haben wir bereits regular verbs und irregular verbs unterschieden. Irregular verbs haben auch für das Past Tense besondere Formen, die wir lernen müssen. Das ist im Deutschen ähnlich: lachen — lachte ist regelmäßig (Englisch: laugh — laughed), aber trinken — trank (Englisch: drink — drank) ist unregelmäßig.
Wir finden die Past forms der Irregular Verbs als Part 2 in der Liste der unregelmäßigen Verben (List of Irregular Verbs, p. 216). Selber üben können wir sie mit Hilfe der Übungen: Test your Irregular Verbs, p. 212.

1 C A story about a day in the city

There are a lot of things you or your friends can do in the city: go to a cinema, buy a ticket and see a nice (or a bad) film, get up and leave the cinema, go and eat a Hamburger in a cafeteria, stand in the street and watch people ... and then come home late.
Now it's your turn. Write a story about a day in the city.
You can start like this:

Last Friday I went to the centre with my friend ... We ...

Exercises

1 What do they usually do? What did they do yesterday?

Example:

Peter goes to school every day, but yesterday he ... to the cinema.
Peter goes to school every day, but yesterday he **went** to the cinema.

Now say what these boys and girls usually do and what they did yesterday.

1 Susan buys an ice-cream every day, but last Sunday she ... 5 biscuits.
2 Tom takes the bus to school, but last Wednesday he ... a taxi.
3 Bert usually comes home early, but last week he ... home late.
4 Mr Miller gets up at seven o'clock in the morning, but last Sunday he ... at 8 o'clock.
5 The teacher often leaves school at 4 o'clock, but last Tuesday he ... school at 8 o'clock.
6 Every Sunday Father eats a piece of cake, but last Sunday he ... 2 pieces of cake.
7 When Peter leaves the house he usually says good-bye, but yesterday he ... cheerio.
8 In the afternoon Tom usually begins his homework at 5 o'clock, but last Thursday he ... at 4 o'clock.

2 What did you do yesterday?

Ask your friends/teacher what they did yesterday. Use the following questions:

1 When did you get up yesterday?
2 What did you have for breakfast?
3 When did you leave the house?
4 What did you learn at school?
5 Where did you sit in the classroom?

Ask more questions:

6 you / to come by bus
7 What / you / to eat at school
8 You / to buy some pop records of Wolle Kriwanek
9 When / you / to go home
10 You / to watch TV last night

3 Thieves!

It was twelve o'clock when Peter came home from the international party at his school. Suddenly he saw three men with big bags. They went into a wonderful big house. Peter jumped behind a tree and watched the house. The lights went on and Peter saw that the three men were taking everything. He watched the thieves for five minutes and then he crossed the street and called the police. Ten minutes later three police cars arrived at the house. The policemen stood behind the trees in the garden and waited.
At twenty past twelve the thieves opened the door, looked into the garden and then across the street and left the house. Suddenly all the policemen came from behind the trees and the inspector said: "Hands up!" Then they took the thieves to the police station. The inspector seemed very pleased and thanked Peter for his help.

When Peter came home he was very tired. He only told his sister: "I've helped the police a lot today." But his sister wanted to know everything. So she asked him a lot of questions.

What were her questions? Who can ask one or more questions about each sentence in the story?

Begin your questions with:

When did you/he/they ...
Where did you/he/they ...
Why did you ...
What did you ...

4 How many verbs do you know?

Look at these forms of the irregular verbs:

say	said	said
go	went	gone
buy	bought	bought
eat	ate	eaten
come	came	come
get up	got up	got up
leave	left	left
see	saw	seen
take	took	taken
sit	sat	sat
find	found	found
be	was	been
begin	began	begun
make	made	made
do	did	done
stand	stood	stood
think	thought	thought
have	had	had

Work with your partner:

a) One of you closes his book. Your friend looks at the list and says for example: took. Now you have to say without looking at the list: take, took, taken

b) Do you know the German translation for these forms?

c) Der Lehrer schreibt eine der Formen an die Tafel. Einer aus der Klasse ergänzt die fehlenden zwei Formen und schreibt eine neue Form eines Verbs an. Er läßt dabei die erste, zweite oder dritte Spalte frei, so daß sie von einem anderen Schüler aus der Klasse ergänzt werden kann.

d) Can you make sentences with these forms?

Examples:

1 Every day I go to school. (Present Tense)
2 Yesterday I went to school. (Past Tense)
3 Have you ever gone to the cinema? (Present Perfect Tense)

Verwende für Sätze mit Verben aus Spalte 1 folgende Ausdrücke:
always, usually, every morning, every Sunday, often, never ...

Verwende für Sätze mit Verben aus Spalte 2 folgende Ausdrücke:
yesterday, last week, last Thursday, in my holidays ...

Verwende für Sätze mit Verben aus Spalte 3 Ausdrücke wie:
ever, never, already, just, (not) yet

14 HDYD CS 2 Textbook 42920

Vocabulary Definitions

a

Today I'm going to the cinema. Yesterday I . . . to the cinema, too.	Heute gehe ich ins Kino. Gestern **ging** ich auch ins Kino.	[went]	**went** (to go)
Today they are sitting at the front. Yesterday they . . . at the front, too.	Heute sitzen sie vorne. Gestern **saßen** sie auch vorne.	[sæt]	**sat** (to sit)
I want to buy a new coat. Oh, I . . . a new coat yesterday.	Ich möchte einen neuen Mantel kaufen. Ach, ich **kaufte** gestern einen neuen Mantel.	[bɔːt]	**bought** (to buy)
When did you eat the meat? Oh, we . . . that yesterday.	Wann hast du das Fleisch gegessen? Das **aßen** wir gestern.	[et]	**ate** (to eat)
When did your friend come? He . . . yesterday.	Wann kam dein Freund? Er **kam** gestern.	[keim]	**came** (to come)
Was he ill? When did he get up? He . . . yesterday.	War er krank? Wann stand er wieder auf? Er **stand** gestern **auf**.	[gɔt'ʌp]	**got up** (to get up)
When did he leave Hamburg? He . . . yesterday.	Wann fuhr er aus Hamburg weg? Er **fuhr** gestern **weg**.	[left]	**left** (to leave)
When did you take these English lessons? I . . . them in the summer.	Wann hast du diese Englischstunden genommen? Ich **nahm** sie im Sommer.	[tuk]	**took** (to take)

b

We left the cinema half an hour . . .	Wir verließen das Kino **vor** einer halben Stunde.	[ə'gəu]	**ago**
They wanted to get the thief, but they did not find him. They . . . to find him.	Sie wollten den Dieb fangen, aber sie fanden ihn nicht. Sie **versuchten**, ihn zu finden.	[traid]	**tried** (to try)
Did they find Heini? Yes, they . . . him in the café.	Haben sie Heini gefunden? Ja, sie **fanden** ihn im Café.	[faund]	**found** (to find)

c

I don't lend my film camera to . . .	Ich verleihe meinen Fotoapparat nicht an **irgend jemanden.**	['enibɔdi]	**anybody**
Can I . . . your camera then?	Kann ich denn deinen Fotoapparat **benutzen**?	[juːz]	**use** (to use)
Can I go to the cinema this afternoon, Dad? . . . I go to the cinema? No, you . . . not.	Kann ich heute nachmittag ins Kino gehen, Vati? **Darf** ich ins Kino gehen? Nein, du **darfst** nicht.	[mei]	**may**
I'm sorry, I must . . .	Es tut mir leid, ich muß es **ablehnen**.	[ri'fjuːz]	**refuse** (to refuse)
You and I, we can take some pictures . . .	Du und ich, wir können **zusammen** ein paar Bilder aufnehmen.	[tə'geðə]	**together**

d

Are you making a speech today? No, I . . . it yesterday.	Hältst du heute eine Rede? Nein, ich **hielt** sie gestern.	[meid]	**made** (to make)
Where did you stand for the school photograph? I . . . in front of the teachers.	Wo standst du bei der Aufnahme für das Schulfoto? Ich **stand** vor den Lehrern.	[stud]	**stood** (to stand)
Ken is the tallest and most . . . boy.	Ken ist der größte und am besten **aussehende** Junge.	['hænsəm]	**handsome**

I can't understand this letter. It's in French. Can you . . . it for me?	Ich verstehe den Brief nicht. Er ist auf Französisch. Kannst du ihn für mich **übersetzen?**	[træns'leit]	**translate** (to translate)
Not always, but . . . Bill welcomes foreign guests.	Nicht immer, aber **manchmal** heißt Bill ausländische Gäste willkommen.	['sʌmtaimz]	**sometimes**
Someone who translates is an . . .	Jemand, der übersetzt, ist ein **Dolmetscher.**	[in'tə:prətə]	**interpreter**
They have arrived from France in England. They have come from a . . . country.	Sie sind aus Frankreich nach England gekommen. Sie sind aus dem **Ausland** gekommen.	['fɔrin]	**foreign**
He can speak German and English. He can speak two . . .	Er kann Deutsch und Englisch. Er kann zwei **Sprachen** sprechen.	['læŋgwidʒiz]	**languages**
Behind Bill you will perhaps see Gwen. You will . . . Gwen.	Hinter Bill wirst du vielleicht Gwen sehen. Du wirst Gwen **bemerken.**	['nəutis]	**notice** (to notice)
The opposite of 'stupid' is . . .	Das Gegenteil von 'dumm' ist **‚schlau/klug'.**	['klevə]	**clever**

e

The first lesson begins at eight. And yesterday the first lesson . . . at eight, too.	Die erste Stunde fängt um acht an. Und gestern **fing** die erste Stunde auch um acht **an.**	[bi'gæn]	**began** (to begin)
He has shops in Germany, France and England. His shops are . . .	Er hat Läden in Deutschland, Frankreich und England. Seine Läden sind **international.**	[intə'næʃnəl]	*international*
He is my very good friend. Our . . . is a very good thing.	Er ist ein sehr guter Freund von mir. Unsere **Freundschaft** ist eine tolle Sache.	['frendʃip]	**friendship**
He has a lot of good records. He has . . . good records.	Er hat sehr viele gute Schallplatten. Er hat **eine Menge** guter Schallplatten.	['plenti‿əv]	**plenty of**
He is clever and . . . Maths.	Er ist klug und **gut in** Mathe.	['gud‿ət]	**good at**
Gerd's English was no good. It was very bad. Belinda's German was . . . than his English.	Gerds Englisch war nicht gut. Es war sehr schlecht. Belindas Deutsch war **noch schlechter** als sein Englisch.	['i:ven 'wə:s]	**even worse**
They danced from seven to eleven. They danced . . .	Sie tanzten von sieben bis elf. Sie tanzten **den ganzen Abend.**	[ɔ:l 'i:vniŋ]	**all evening**
I think a foreign language is very useful. And yesterday I . . . that too.	Ich denke, eine Fremdsprache ist sehr nützlich. Und das **dachte** ich gestern auch schon.	[θɔ:t]	**thought** (to think)

Exercise 3

. . . he saw three men with big bags.	**Plötzlich** sah er 3 Männer mit großen Taschen.	['sʌdnli]	**suddenly**

Listening dialogue texts and games

Unit 8: A game with the tape-recorder

Haven't you got a tape-recorder? Well, make these noises for your pupils then.

1 He has just knocked at the door.
2 He has just opened a door.
3 He has just closed a book.
4 He has just started the car.
5 He has just washed his hands.
6 He has just returned to the room.
7 He has just rushed into the room.
8 He has just kissed his girl-friend.

R II: A game with the tape-recorder

1 Look at Susan and Betty. What are their skirts like?
2 And what about their hair?
3 What about their shoes?
4 Look at their baskets. Compare them. (Vergleiche die zwei Körbe!)
5 Look at Tom and Betty. Is Tom taller than Betty?
6 Now look at Betty and Susan. Is Susan taller than Betty?
7 The two boys love good food. They always eat chocolate. Compare the two boys.
8 Now look at the two boys' jackets. Compare their jackets.
9 What about the boys' age?
10 What about their shoes?

Unit 10: A game with the tape-recorder

Haven't you got a tape-recorder? Well, make these noises in class then.

1	What has happened to Susan?	Susan has fallen out of bed.
2	What has Betty done?	Betty has bought four tickets.
3	What has Betty just done?	Betty has just given Susan a ticket.
4	What has Eileen done?	Eileen has bought three ice-creams.
5	What has Eileen just done?	Eileen has just eaten David's apple.
6	What about Dadid's purse?	It has fallen into the water.
7	What about Tom?	Tom has (just) come.

Unit 11: German food is too good

Eileen: Where are you going this afternoon, Carol?
Carol: I'm going into the centre of Hamburg to a big department store. I need a new skirt.
Eileen: Are you going by tube?
Carol: No, I'm going to cycle on Herr Bäcker's bike.
Eileen: Why do you have to buy another new skirt? You've got a lovely new skirt already.
Carol: I know. It's the German Torte and Schlagsahne. My skirt is too small for me now.
Eileen: That's silly. I can make it bigger for you. Show me. Yes, that's all right. But you mustn't eat any more Torte.
Carol: Thanks a lot, Eileen.
Eileen: You can buy me a big ice-cream at the shop opposite the post office when I've finished your skirt.
Carol: Is ice-cream as bad as Torte, do you think?
Eileen: No, I don't think so.

Test your irregular verbs

Dies ist ein Übungsprogramm, mit dem du leicht die wichtigsten 20 unregelmäßigen Verben lernen und selbst korrigieren kannst. Du kannst dir selber Nachhilfestunden geben und dein eigener Lehrer sein. Wenn du mit Freunden zusammenarbeitest, macht es sicher noch mehr Spaß.

Das Programm verläuft so:

Es besteht aus 10 Verben mit Ergänzungen, aus denen du nach der Vorlage des Beispiels Fragen und Antworten bildest. Danach unterstreichst du die Formen der unregelmäßigen Verben. Dann kontrollierst du, ob sie richtig sind. Du findest sie in der List of Irregular Verbs (Seite 216). Die Form für das Present Perfect Tense findest du in Spalte 3 (Part 3), die für das Past Tense in Spalte 2. Das Nachschlagen ist zwar ein wenig mühsam, aber dabei lernst du nebenbei auch andere Verben, während du das richtige suchst. Am Ende zählst du zusammen: wenn beide Formen richtig sind, gibst du dir einen Punkt.

Acht Punkte und mehr: sehr gut (bei 8 und 9 Punkten verbesserst du den Fehler)
Sechs und sieben Punkte: gut (aber die Fehler mußt du verbessern).

Fünf Punkte und weniger: nicht so gut (am besten, du versuchst, mit dem zweiten Teil des Programms, das die gleichen Verben hat, eine bessere Punktzahl zu erreichen).

Du solltest solange zwischen den beiden Gruppen mit den gleichen Verben wechseln, bis du die Verben sicher kannst, mindestens ein ‚gut' erreicht hast. Dann kannst du den zweiten Teil versuchen.

Nach einiger Zeit solltest du das Programm wiederholen und prüfen, ob du die Verbformen auch behalten hast.

Erster Teil

A. *Example:* **Have** you ever **seen** a Western film?
Certainly, yesterday I **saw** a Western film.

1 sell tickets for a pop concert
2 read our school magazine
3 steal apples from our neighbour's garden
4 teach your brother table tennis
5 lose your purse
6 wear a tie
7 write a letter to the USA
8 throw a stone into the North Sea
9 hear a German folksong
10 come home after 8 o'clock

B. *Example:* Yesterday I **saw** the Beatles on TV.
I **have** never **seen** the Beatles on TV.

1 sell our school magazine
2 read an English newspaper
3 steal a pencil from my friend
4 teach my sister an English song
5 lose my bus ticket
6 wear white jeans
7 write a letter to my American friend
8 throw a ball into our neighbour's garden
9 hear the Queen on the radio
10 come home from school after tea

Zweiter Teil

A. *Example:* I have never written a letter to my teacher.
But I wrote a letter to my teacher last weekend.

1 sleep in a hotel
2 run the 400 metres
3 stand on Westminster Bridge in London
4 take my best friend home for tea.
5 tell my friends about our dog
6 shake hands with a pop-star
7 meet a girl from the USA
8 leave the cinema before the end of the film
9 give my sister a present
10 bring my guitar to a party

B. *Example:* Yesterday I wrote a letter to my grandmother.
I have never written a letter to my grandmother.

1 sleep on a boat
2 run without shoes in the street
3 stand on the roof of our house
4 take my friend to a party
5 tell my teacher about my English friend
6 shake hands with our new teacher
7 meet a pop star
8 leave my English books at school
9 give my grandmother a birthday present
10 bring my cat to school with me

Grammar index

ist, wie in CS 1, eine Übersicht, die dir helfen soll, grammatische Erklärungen und Übungen zu finden, wenn du sie in der Klasse oder auch für dich wiederholen willst. Natürlich ist diese Tabelle nicht vollständig: wir haben das ganz leichte weggelassen, nur das aufgenommen, was du gelegentlich wiederholen, nachlesen oder miteinander vergleichen mußt, wenn du sicher werden willst im Englischsprechen und -schreiben.

List of irregular verbs

Part 1	Part 2	Part 3
am (→ be)	was/were	been
bring	brought	brought
choose	chose	chosen
come	came	come
cost	cost	cost
do	did	done
draw	drew	drawn
drink	drank	drunk
eat	ate	eaten
find	found	found
forget	forgot	forgotten
get	got	got
give	gave	given
go	went	gone
have	had	had
hear	heard	heard
know	knew	known
lay	laid	laid
leave	left	left
lend	lent	lent
let	let	let
lie (liegen)	lay	lain
lose	lost	lost
make	made	made
mean	meant	meant
meet	met	met
overtake	overtook	overtaken
pay	paid	paid
put	put	put
read [i:]	read [e]	read [e]
run	ran	run
say	said	said
see	saw	seen
sell	sold	sold
send	sent	sent
shake	shook	shaken
sleep	slept	slept
speak	spoke	spoken
steal	stole	stolen
stand	stood	stood
take	took	taken
teach	taught	taught
tell	told	told
think	thought	thought
throw	threw	thrown
understand	understood	understood
wake	woke (waked)	waked (woken, woke)
wear	wore	worn
write	wrote	written

Alphabetical vocabulary

Kursiv gedruckte Wörter sind als rezeptives ("recognition") Vokabular zu betrachten.

I = CS I   II = CS II

A

accident II, 7 c
across I, 12 d
afraid (= I'm ~) II, 7 d
after II, 4 b
afternoon (this ~) I, 8 e
again I, 9 b
against II, 5 c
age II, 6 a
ago II, 13 b
to agree II, 2 b
alarm-clock II, 5 b
all II, 2 d
all morning II, 9 a
all evening II, 13 e
all right I, 9 b
to allow II, 8 d
almost II, 9 d
alone II, 8 b
already I, 10 c
always I, 10 b
ambulance II, 7 c
American I, 9 b
angry (= to be ~) II, 5 c
another II, 4 c
to answer II, 6 e
any I, 11 b
anybody II, 13 c
anyone II, 8 b
anything II, 3 d
anywhere II, 10 e
anxious II, 10 e
apple I, 4 c
arm II, 7 c
to arrive I, 7 c
to ask I, 8 Q
to ask about II, 1 e
to ask the way II, 9 c
assistant I, 3 b
as soon as possible II, 9 d
at I, 4 c
at home I, 10 b
at last II, 3 c
at once II, 7 a
aunt II, 7 d
Avenue II, 3 d
away II, 6 e
awful I, 2 d

B

back (= ~ of my taxi) I, 13 c
back (= to be ~) II, 4 e
back (= his ~) II, 7 c
bacon I, 10 e
bad II, 9 a
badly II, 9 a
bag I, 1 c
to bake II, 11 d
baker II, 4 a
ball I, 1 c
ball-point I, 2 c
basket I, 2 c
bath I, 9 a
bathroom I, 10 b
to be I, 1, 2
beautiful II, 6 d
because II, 4 c
bedroom I, 3 a
beer I, 4 a
before II, 9 c
to begin II, 13 e
behind I, 6 c
bell II, 5 b
to believe II, 3 c
beside I, 8 e
big I, 5 c
bike I, 3 a
bill II, 12 b
bird I, 4 d
birthday II, 11 d
biscuit I, 4 d
black I, 1 b
blanket II, 8 a
blazer II, 5 b
block of flats I, 13 b
blue I, 1 b
board I, 2 a
boat II, 1 a
boat-train II, 1 c
book I, 1 b
to borrow II, 11 d
boring II, 12 f
both II, 7 d
bottle I, 11 a
box I, 13 c
boy I, 2 d
bread I, 11 a
breakfast I, 10 b
to bring I, 4 a
broken II, 7 c
brother I, 3 a
brown I, 2 c
building II, 11 c
bull I, 7 a
bus I, 7 c
busy I, 4 a
butter I, 12 a
to buy I, 11 a
by II, 6 d
by train II, 9 d
bye-bye I, 1 c

C

cabin II, 10 d
café II, 9 b
cafeteria I, 8 c
cake I, 8 b
calendar II, 4 a
to call II, 11 b
call-box II, 6 d
to be called II, 8 e
camera II, 6 e
can I, 8 a
cap I, 4 b
car I, 2 c
car ferry II, 10 a
car park I, 8 d
careful I, 6 e
carefully II, 9 c
cat I, 2 c
cathedral II, 3 c
centre II, 11 c
chair I, 2 b
chalk I, 2 c
change, small ~ I, 12 b
cheap I, 9 a
cheese I, 9 c
chest-of-drawers I, 13 b
chicken I, 7 a
child I, 7 a
children I, 7 a
children's home II, 7 d
chips I, 8 e
chocolate I, 8 c
to choose II, 2 d
cinema II, 11 d
city II, 11 c
classroom I, 2 a
to clean I, 8 c
clerk II, 1 e
clever II, 13 d
clock II, 5 b
to close II, 6 e
clothes II, 11 d
cloudy II, 12 d
club I, 10 a

to have (= ~ dinner) I, 6 c
to have got I, 5 b
to have to I, 10 a
head II, 8 c
head girl II, 10 e
headmaster I, 7 c
to hear II, 2 b
heavy I, 13 c
hello I, 1 a
help I, 6 e
helpful II, 12 c
here I, 2 a
here you are I, 12 a
holiday II, 3 d
home (= at ~) I, 7 b
homework I, 4 a
honestly II, 7 a
to hope II, 6 b
horse I, 7 a
hospital II, 4 c
hot I, 8 c
hotel I, 5 a
hour II, 11 b
house I, 2 b
how do you do I, 2 b
how are you I, 2 d
how many I, 7 Q
how much I, 8 b
how old I, 3 c
hungry I, 8 e
to hurry up I, 10 c
husband I, 13 c

I

ice-cream I, 8 b
idea II, 6 c
I'd like I, 12 a
ill I, 8 a
important II, 5 b
in I, 2 a
in front of I, 6 c
to injure II, 7 d
inside I, 6 c
instead of II, 12 c
interesting I, 9 b
international II, 13 e
interpreter II, 13 d
to interview I, 10 d
into I, 6 c
to introduce II, 4 d
to invite II, 7 a
invitation card II, 4 a
Irish stew I, 9 c
it I, 1 b

J

jeans II, 2 c
job I, 5 a
journey II, 12 c
juice I, 8 b
to jump I, 6 c
just (= only) I, 10 e
just (= gerade) I, 12 c

K

key I, 12 d
kilometre I, 10 e
kind II, 9 a
kiss II, 3 b
kitchen I, 3 a
to knock II, 4 c
to know I, 10 e

L

ladder I, 6 d
lane I, 3 b
language II, 13 d
large II, 5 b
last II, 5 c
late I, 10 b
later I, 10 c
to laugh II, 2 d
lawn I, 13 b
to lay the table I, 6 a
to leave (trans.) I, 13 c
left (= on the ~) I, 5 c
leg I, 10 c
lemonade I, 11 c
to lend I, 9 d
lesson II, 5 d
to let II, 9 d
let's I, 11 b
letter II, 5 c
to lie (= liegen) I, 10 d
lifeboat II, 10 d
lift (= Fahrstuhl) I, 9 a
to lift II, 4 d
to give a lift II, 9 b
like (= what's it~) II, 1 e
like (= fair ~ Inge) II, 2 d
to like I, 9 c
lion II, 6 d
to listen I, 4 d
litre I, 12 b
to live II, 7 d
living-room I, 2 b
loaf I, 11 a
long II, 2 a
long way II, 9 c
to look I, 1 b
to look (= aussehen) II, 3 a
to look at I, 4 b
to look for I, 6 c
lorry II, 6 e
to lose (= ~ your way) II, 9 c
Lost Property Office II, 1 e
a lot of I, 11 a
Love II, 10 Ex. 4
to love I, 9 b
lovely I, 9 b
lucky I, 11 c
luggage II, 7 b
lunch II, 6 b

M

magazine II, 5 b
to make I, 8 e
man I, 11 c
manager I, 5 a
map I, 2 a
match (= Spiel) I, 10 a
Maths II, 5 c
may II, 13 c
meal II, 2 a
to mean II, 2 a
meat I, 9 c
to meet II, 3 c
men I, 13 b
menu I, 5 c
middle (= in the ~ of) II, 8 a
mile II, 3 d
milk I, 8 b
to mind II, 5 a
minute I, 4 b
mirror I, 13 b
to be missing II, 10 d
mistake II, 8 e
moment II, 8 c
money I, 11 c
month II, 7 d
morning I, 1 c
mother I, 3 a
motorway II, 7 c
to move to I, 13 b
Mum I, 2 d
music II, 12 b
must I, 11 c

N

name I, 2 a
near II, 3 d
nearer II, 3 d
to need I, 11 a
never I, 10 b
new I, 3 c
next II, 6 e
next morning II, 10 a
next-door II, 12 b
next to I, 8 d
nice I, 3 c
night I, 9 a

What do I say?

Was ich sage, wenn

. . . ich etwas nicht verstehe:	I don't understand that. I'm sorry. I don't understand. Why is that?
. . . ich etwas erklärt haben möchte:	Can you explain this word/sentence, please? What does " . . . " mean?
. . . ich etwas wiederholt haben möchte:	Please say that again. Can you repeat that, please? Can you play that again, please?
. . . etwas zu schnell gesprochen wurde:	Not so fast, please That was too fast. I didn't understand. Can you say that slowly, please?
. . . ich nicht weiß, wie ich etwas auf englisch ausdrücken kann:	What's the English for . . .? How do I say that I want to . . .? Can I say this in German, please?
. . . ich etwas übersetzt haben möchte:	Can you translate that, please? Can you say that sentence in German? What's the German for . . . ?
. . . ich wissen will, wie etwas geschrieben wird:	How do you spell that word? Can you write that on the board, please?
. . . ich wissen will, wie etwas ausgesprochen wird:	How do you pronounce this word? Can you say this word for me, please?
. . . ich wissen will, ob etwas in meinem Heft richtig ist:	Can you look at my exercise book? Can you check my homework? Is this right?

. . . es im Zimmer zu laut ist:	There's too much noise. I can't hear.
. . . mein Nachbar mich immer stört:	Leave me alone. I want to concentrate. Don't interrupt me.
. . . ich meine Mitschüler nach ihrer Meinung fragen will:	What do you think of this? Do you agree with that? Do you think this is boring/interesting?
. . . ich meine Meinung sagen will:	I don't like this. This is very difficult/too easy. I think it is silly/funny/exciting/sad. I don't think this is very . . .
. . . ich lieber etwas anderes machen möchte:	I'm fed up with this. Do we really have to do this boring exercise again? Can we go to the language lab? Can't we read a story instead?
. . . ich mich gegen Vorwürfe verteidigen will:	It wasn't me. I wasn't talking. That's not fair. I . . . That's not true. Why have you given me a grade 5?
. . . ich etwas nicht sehen kann:	I can't see. Can you hold that higher, please? I can't see the picture properly.
. . . ich das Fenster öffnen will:	Can I open the window, please?
. . . ich den Raum verlassen möchte:	Can I leave the room, please? I don't feel well. Can I be excused, please? I want to go to the toilet.